This book belongs to......

....

....

Small preview of what's inside

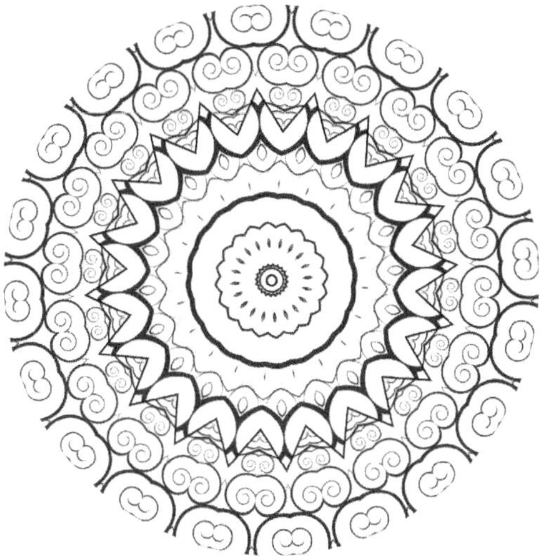
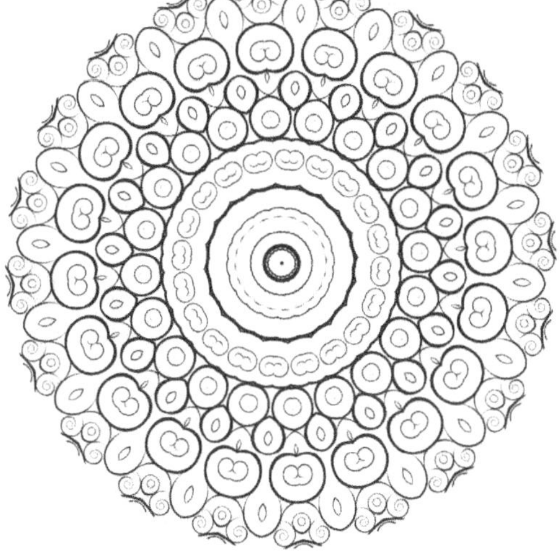
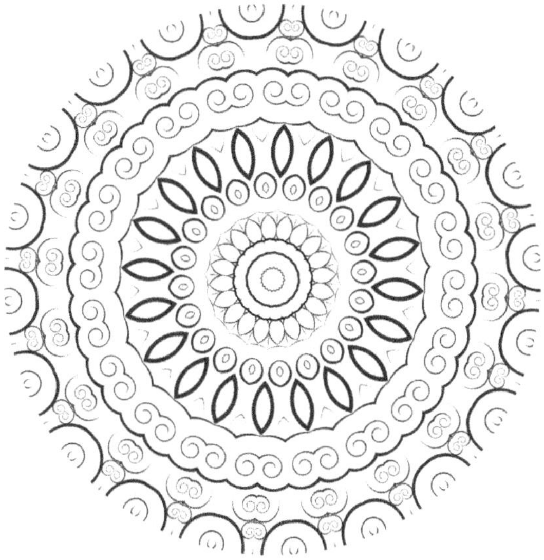
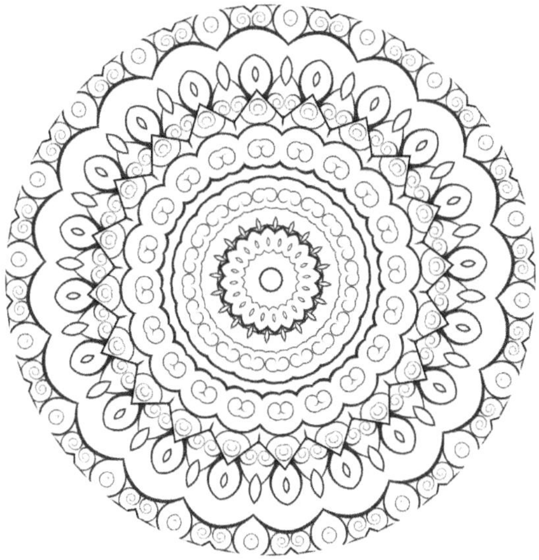
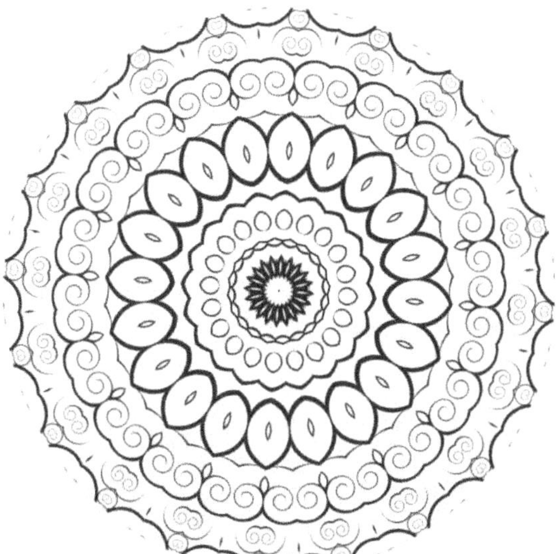
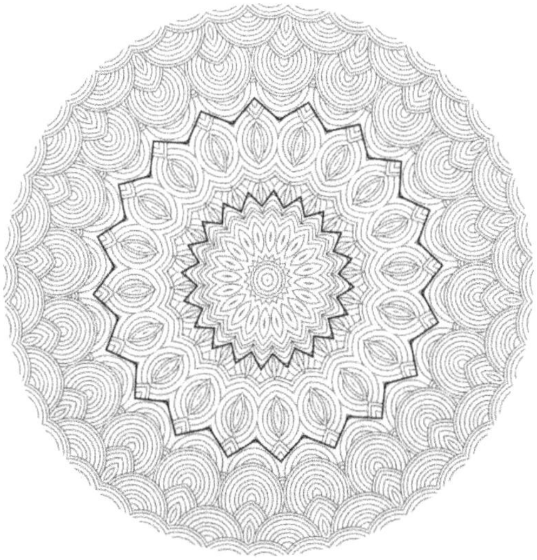

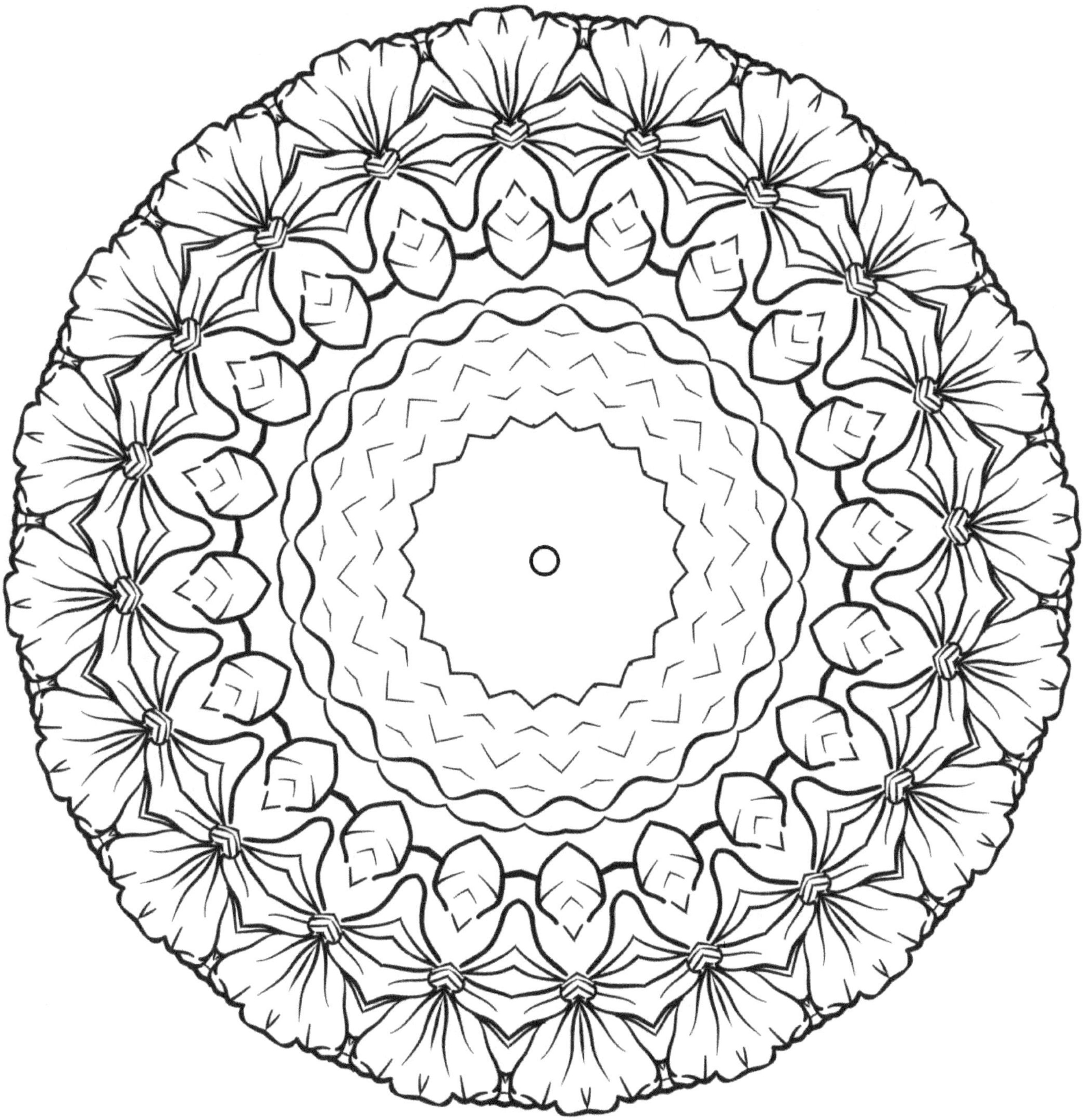

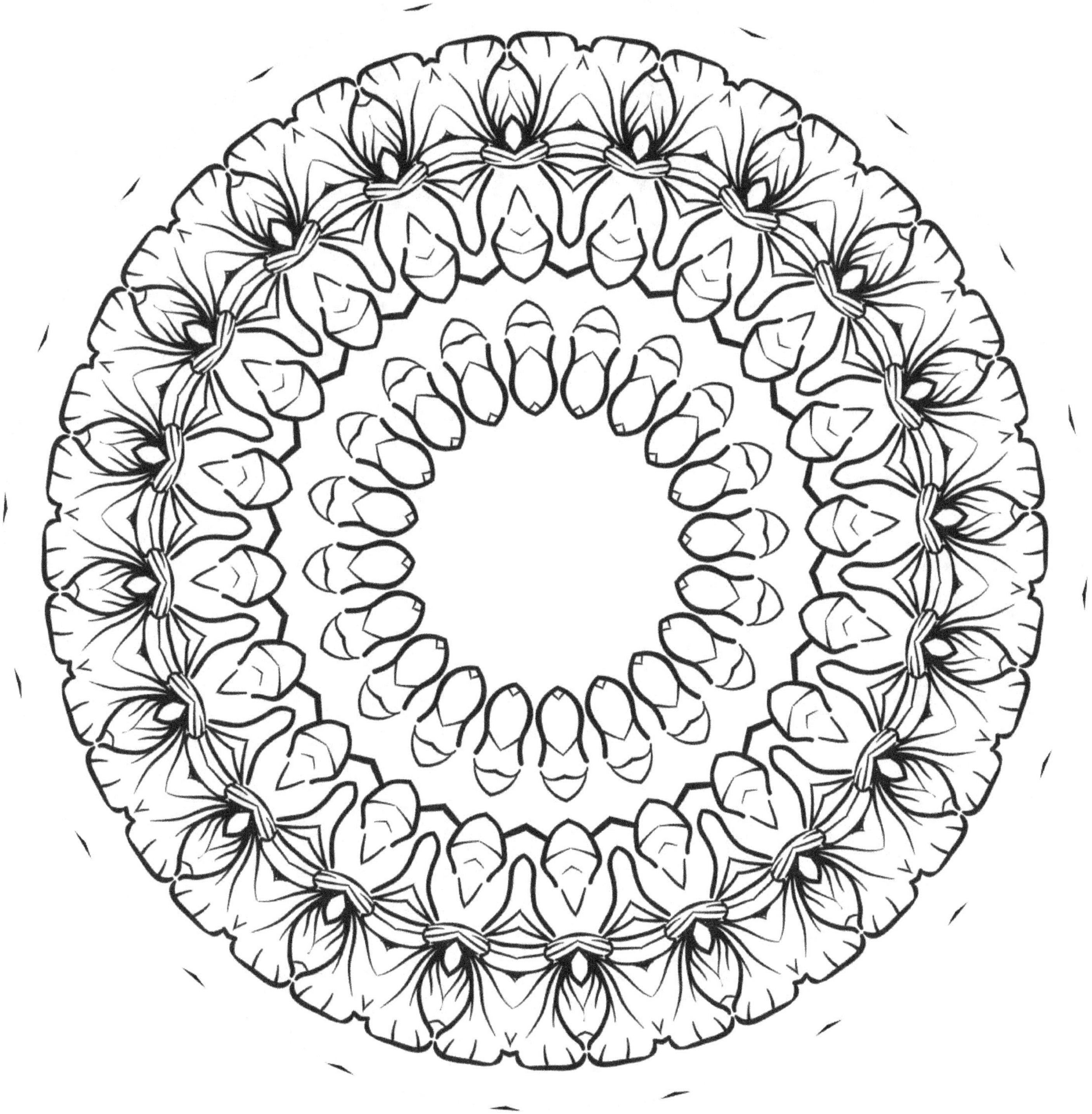

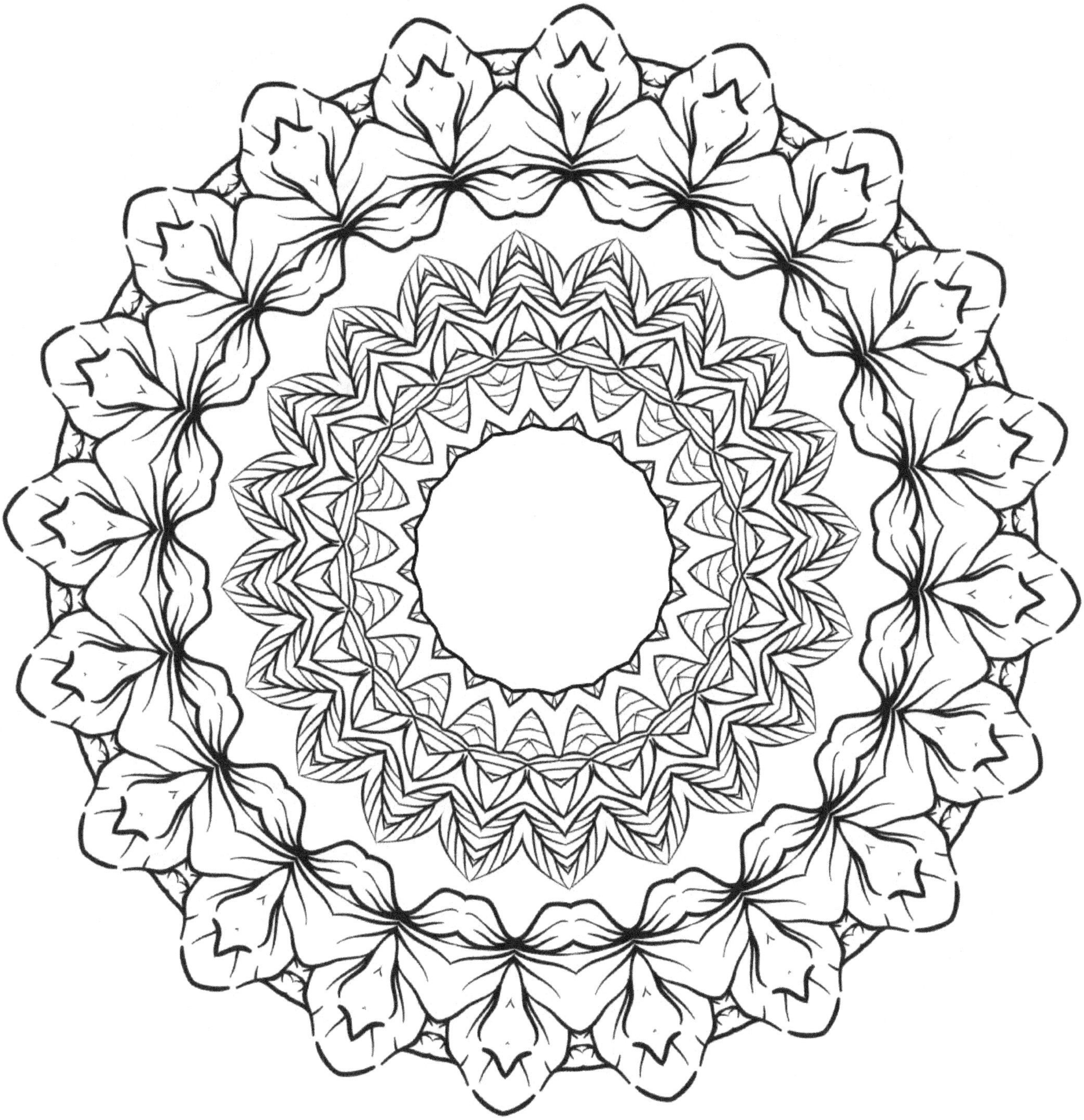

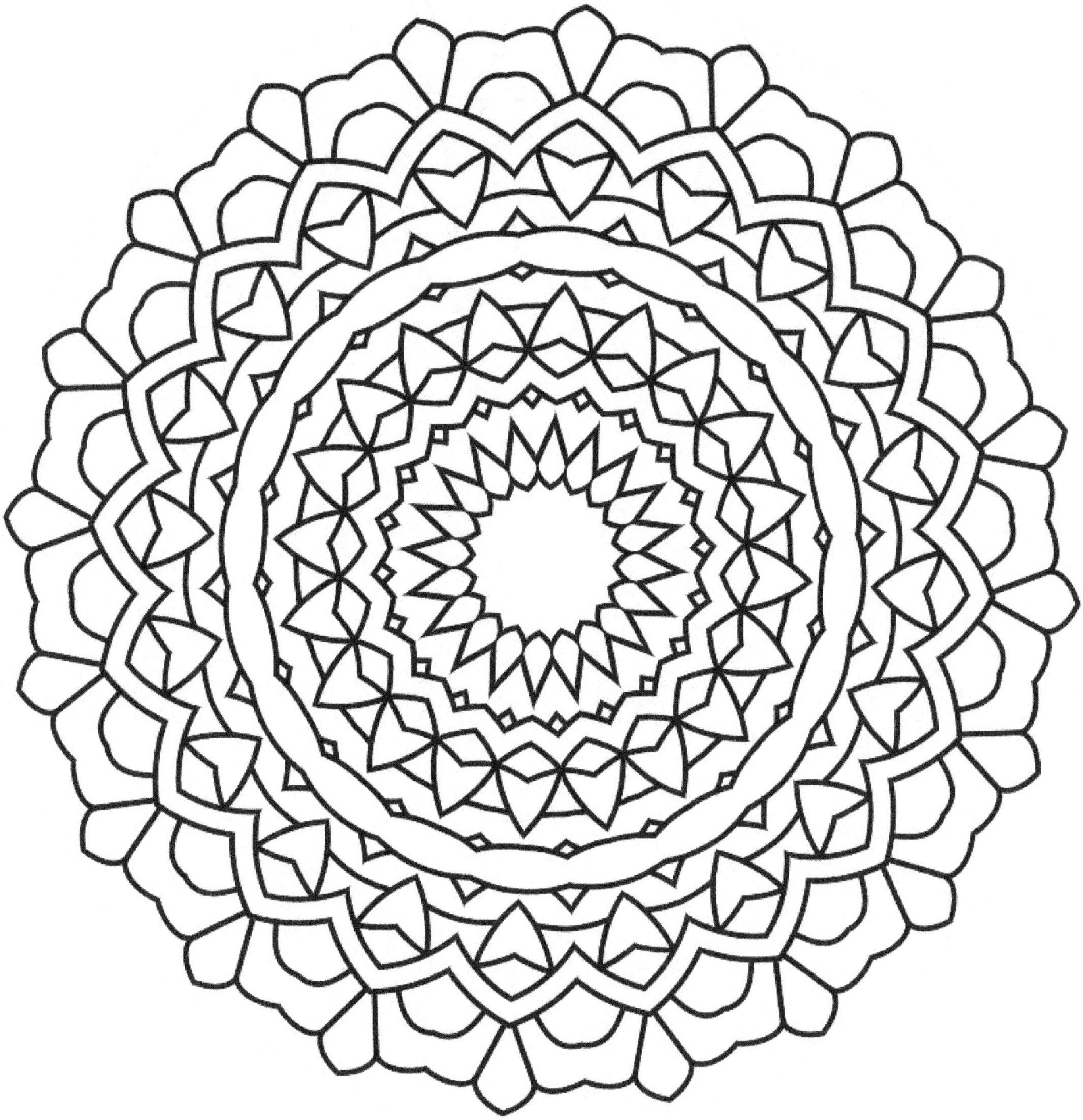

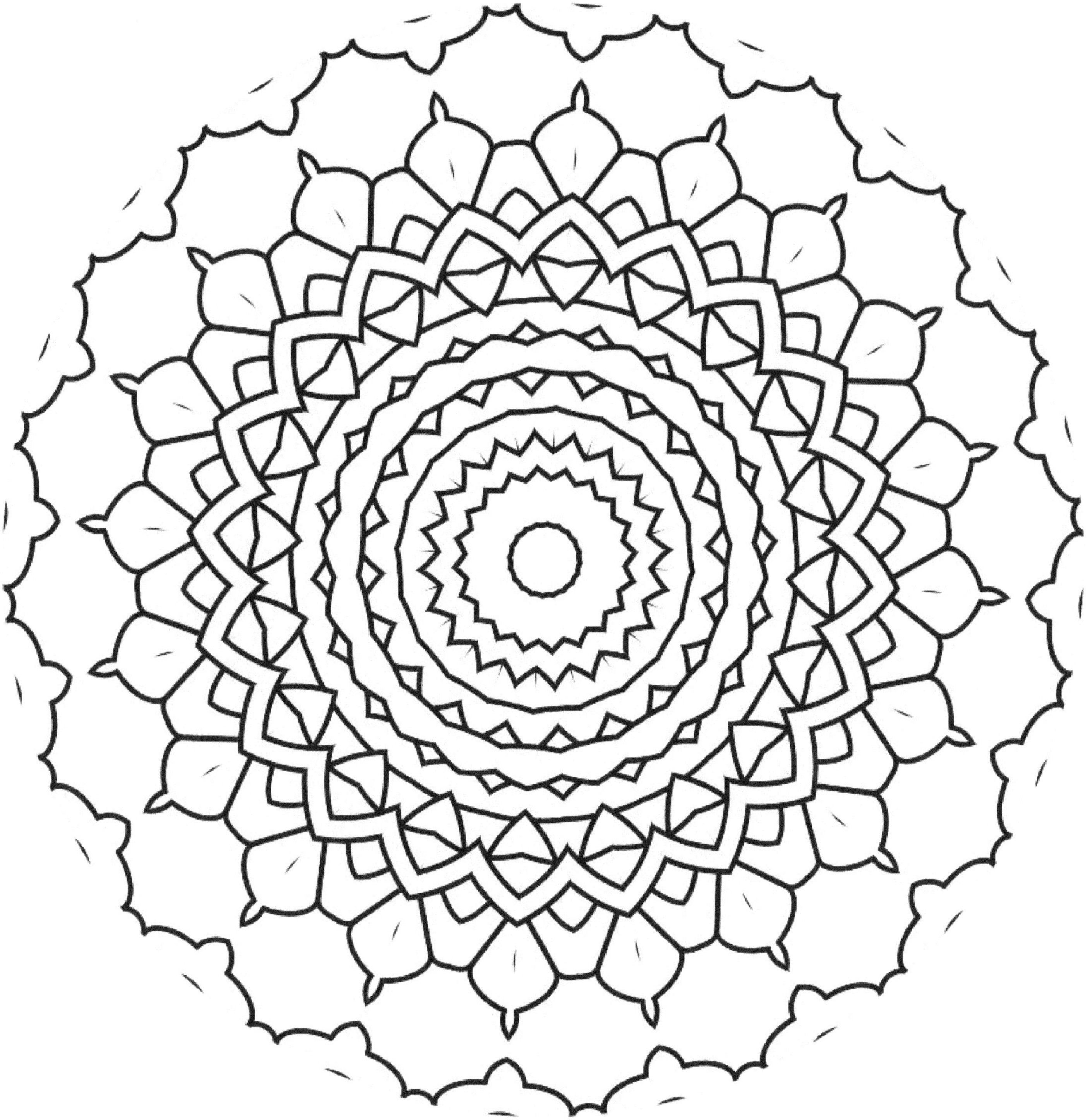

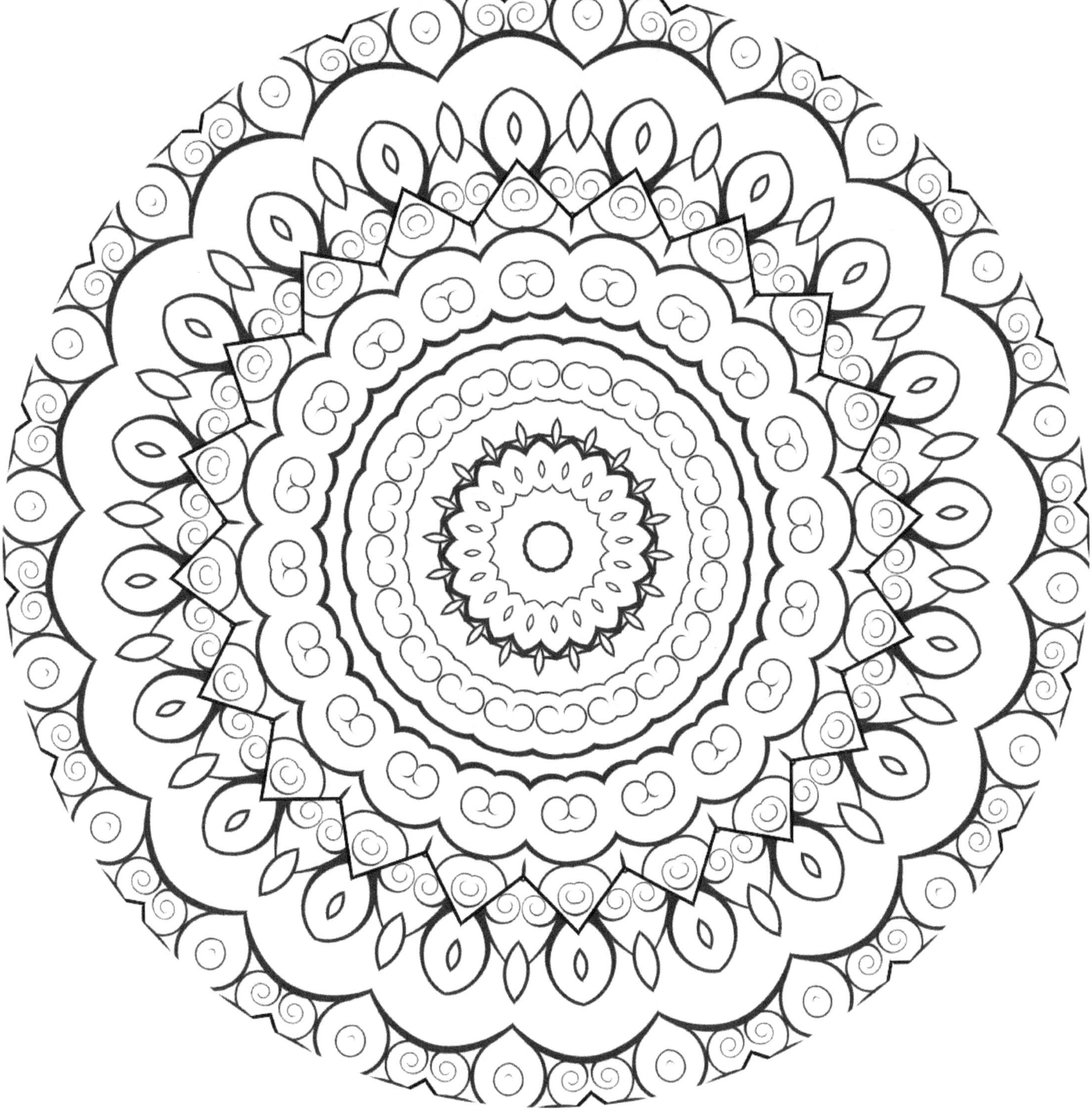

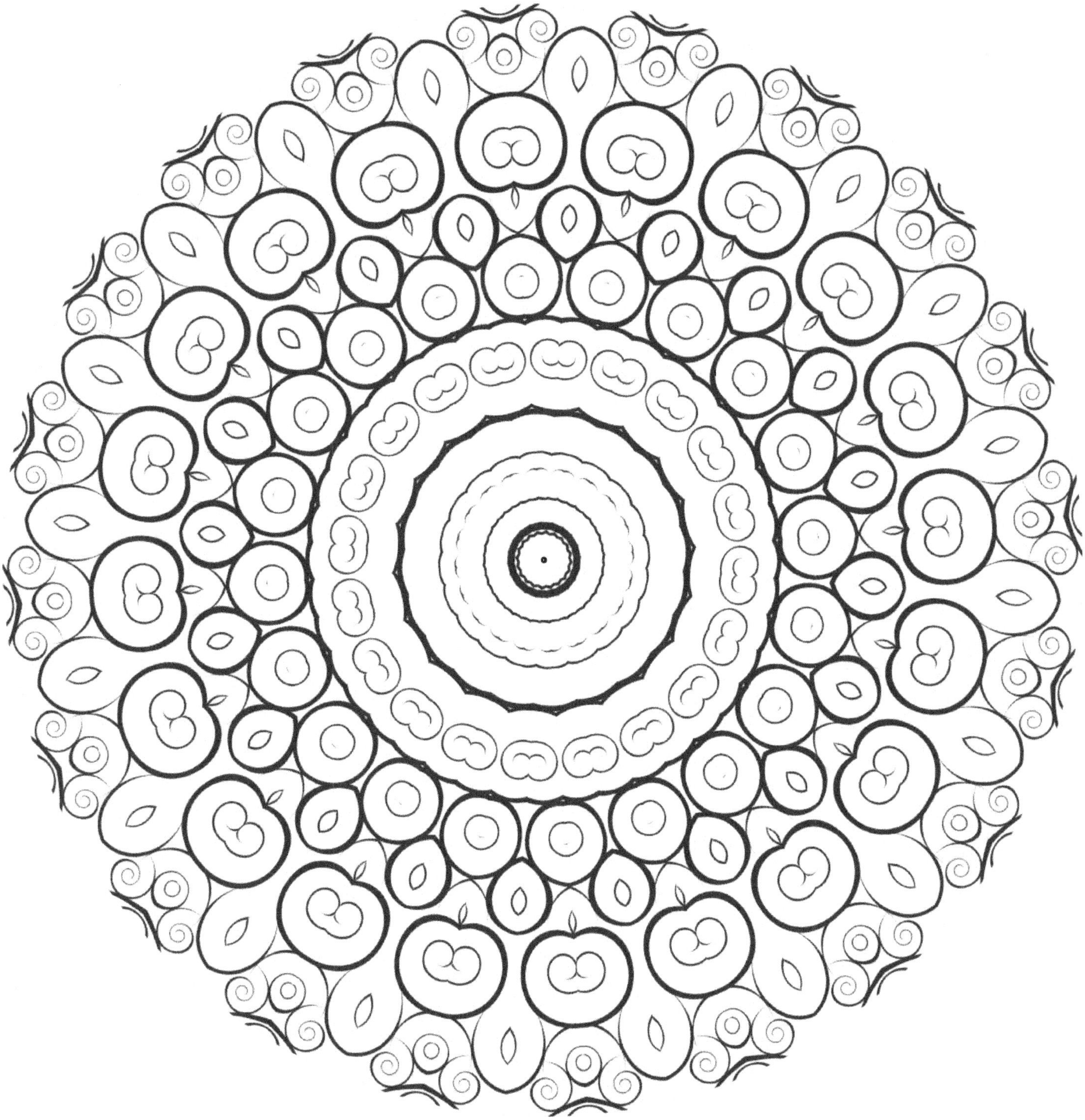

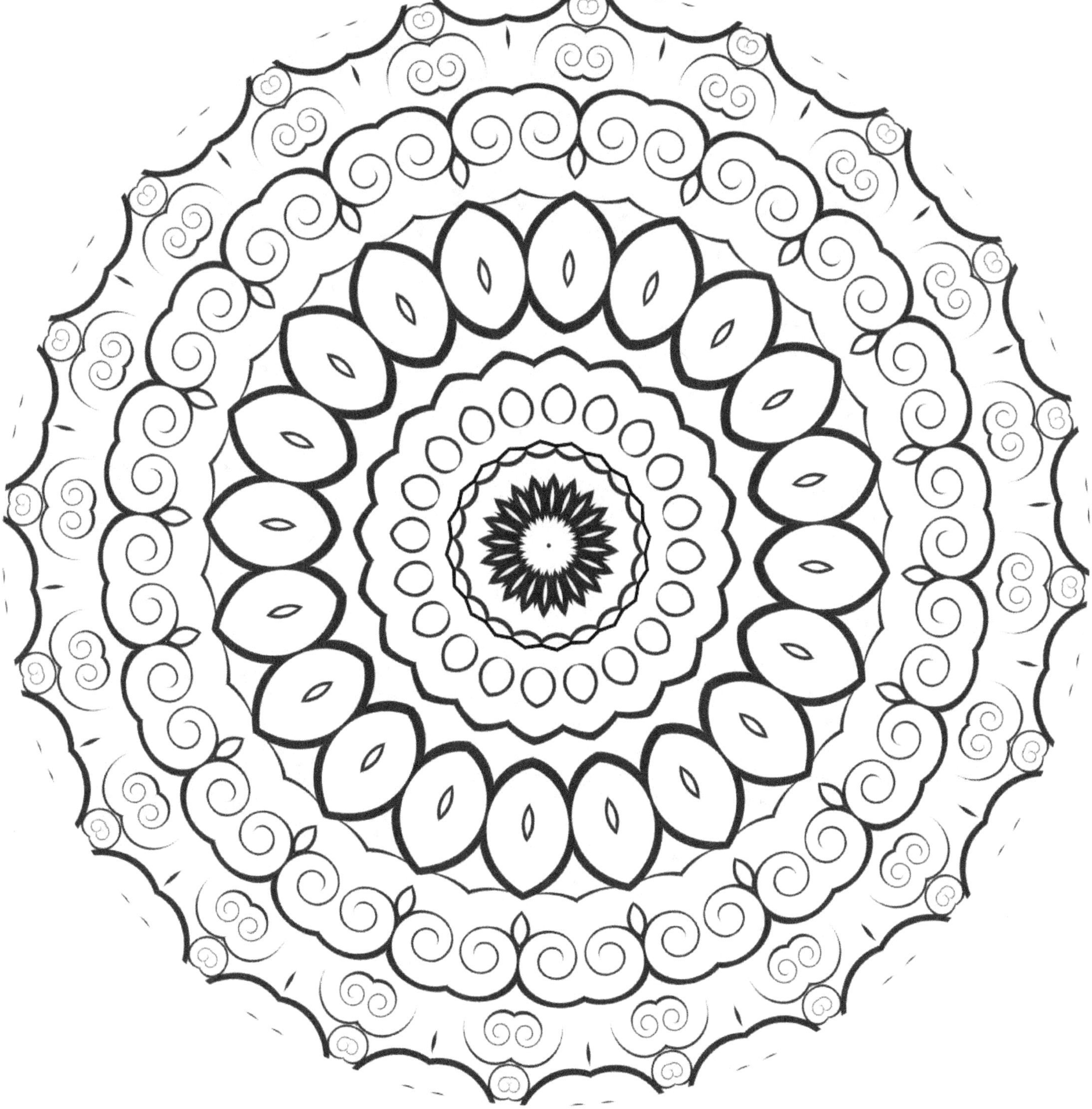

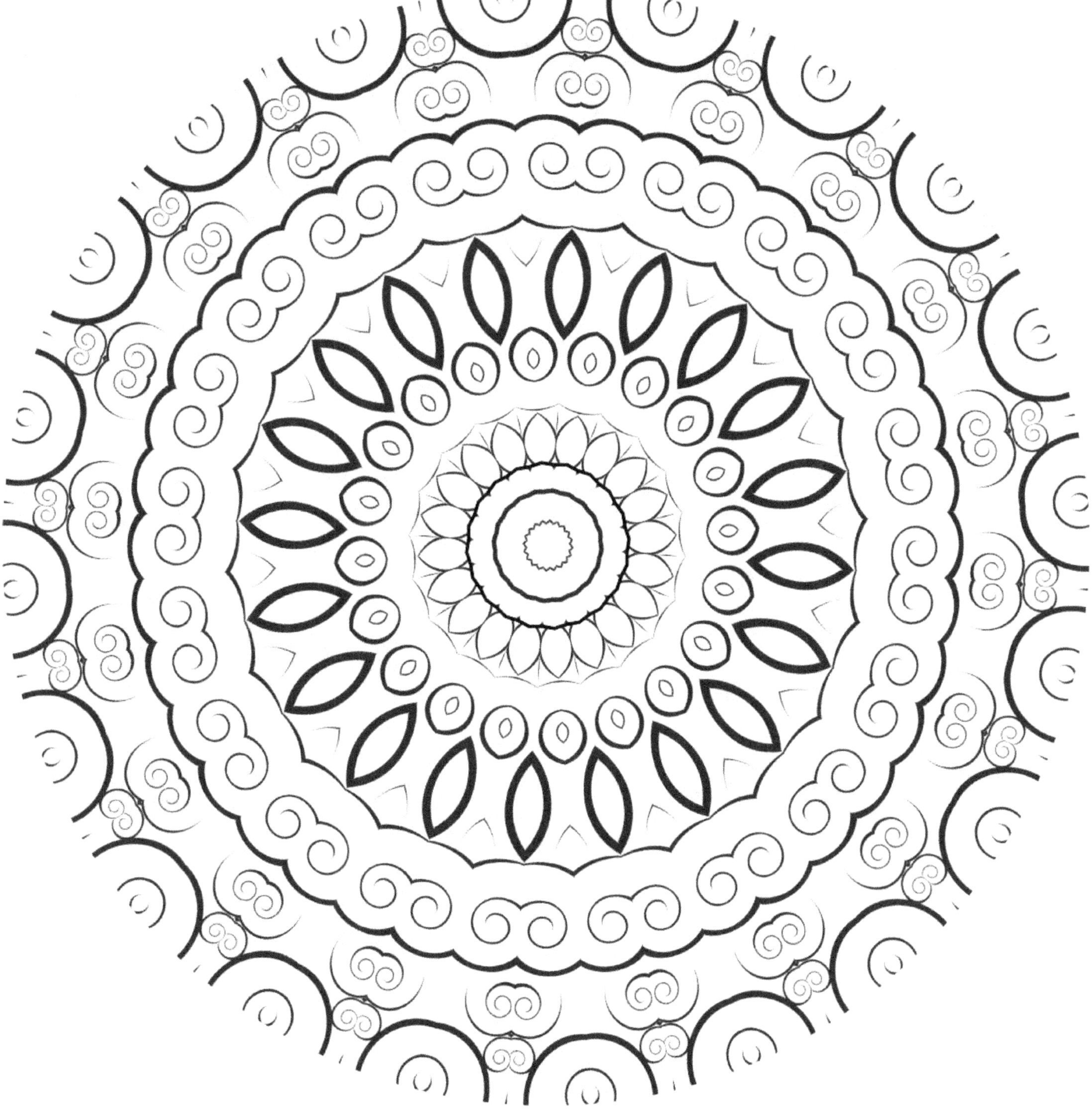

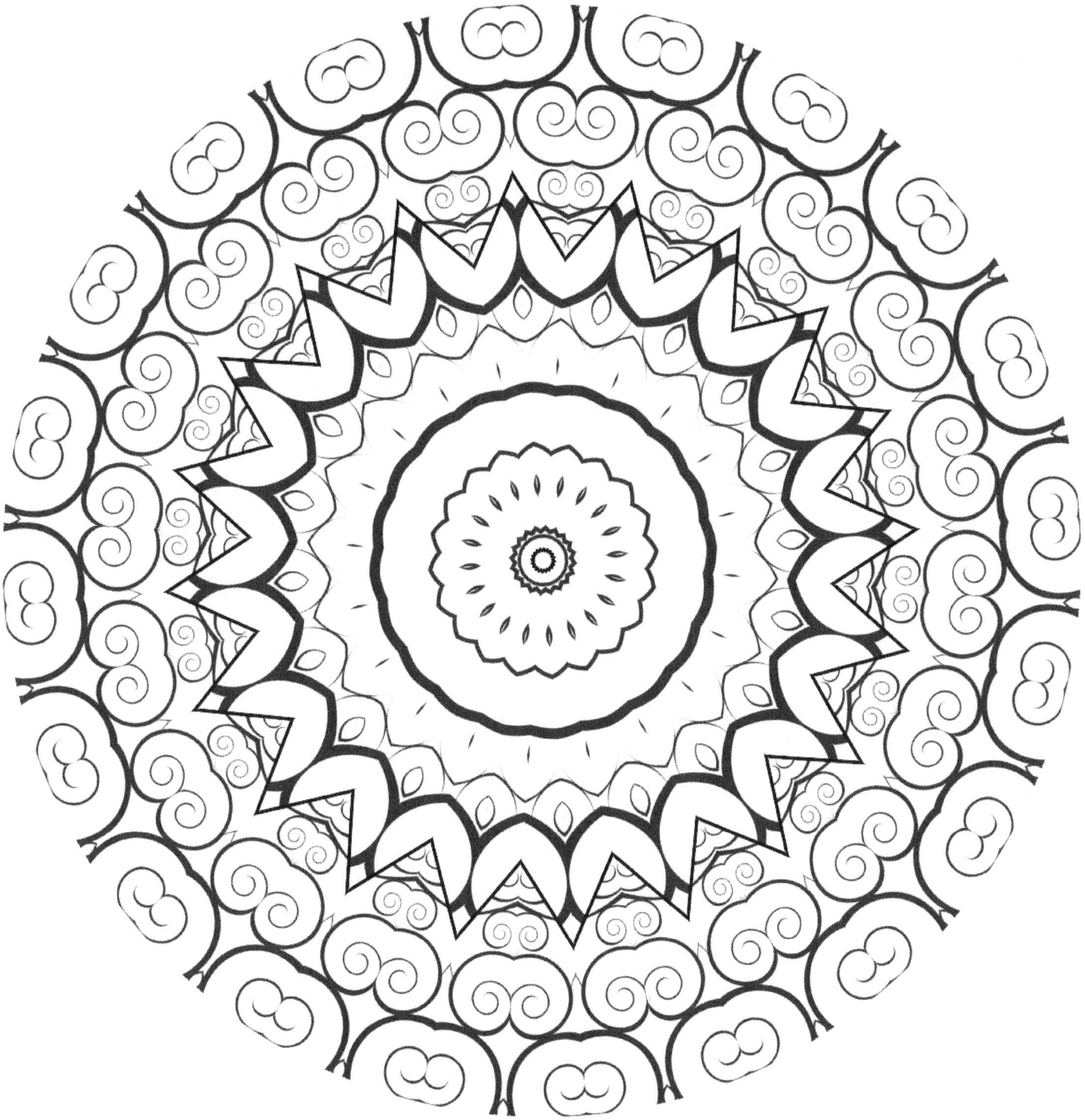

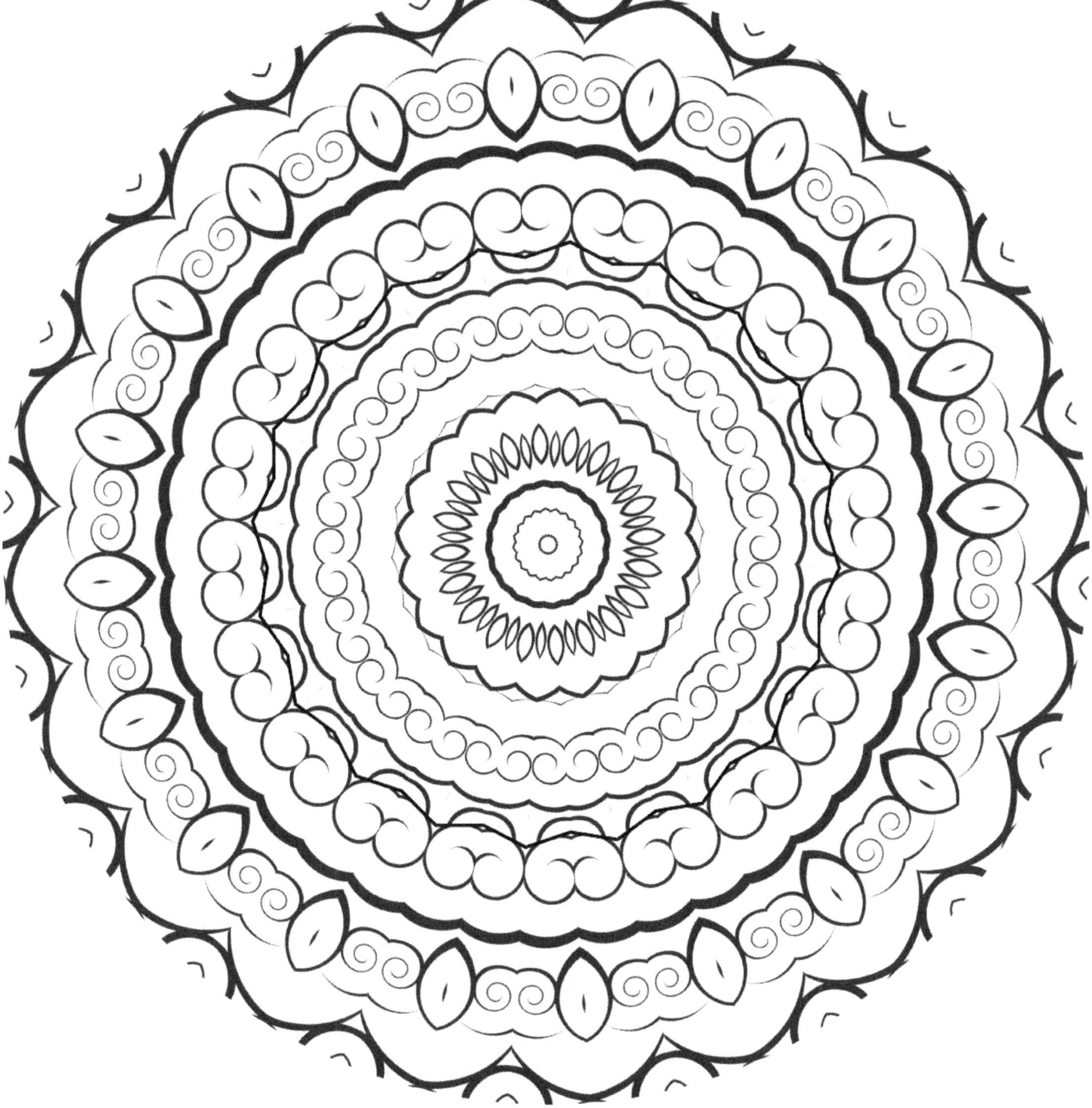

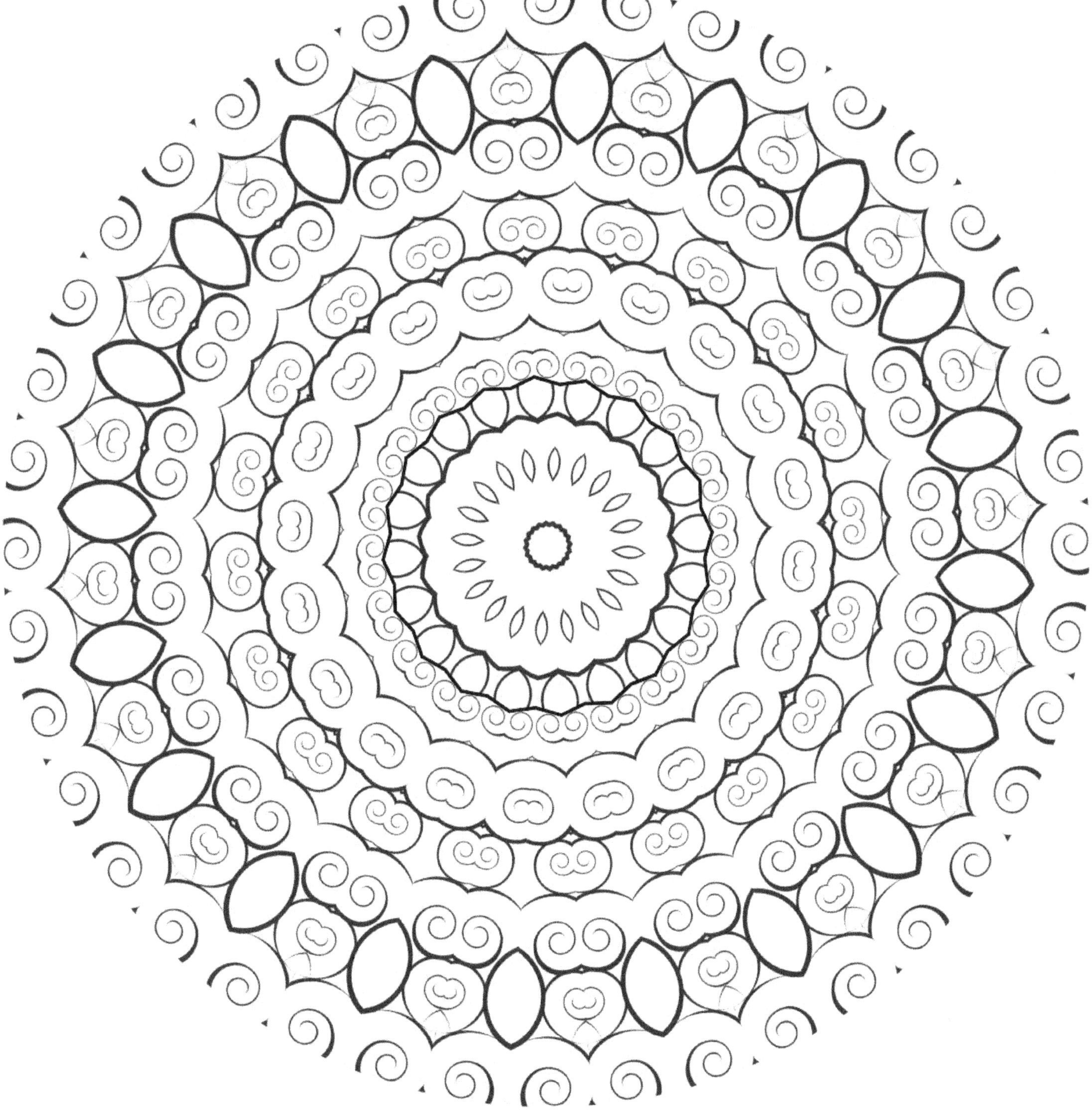

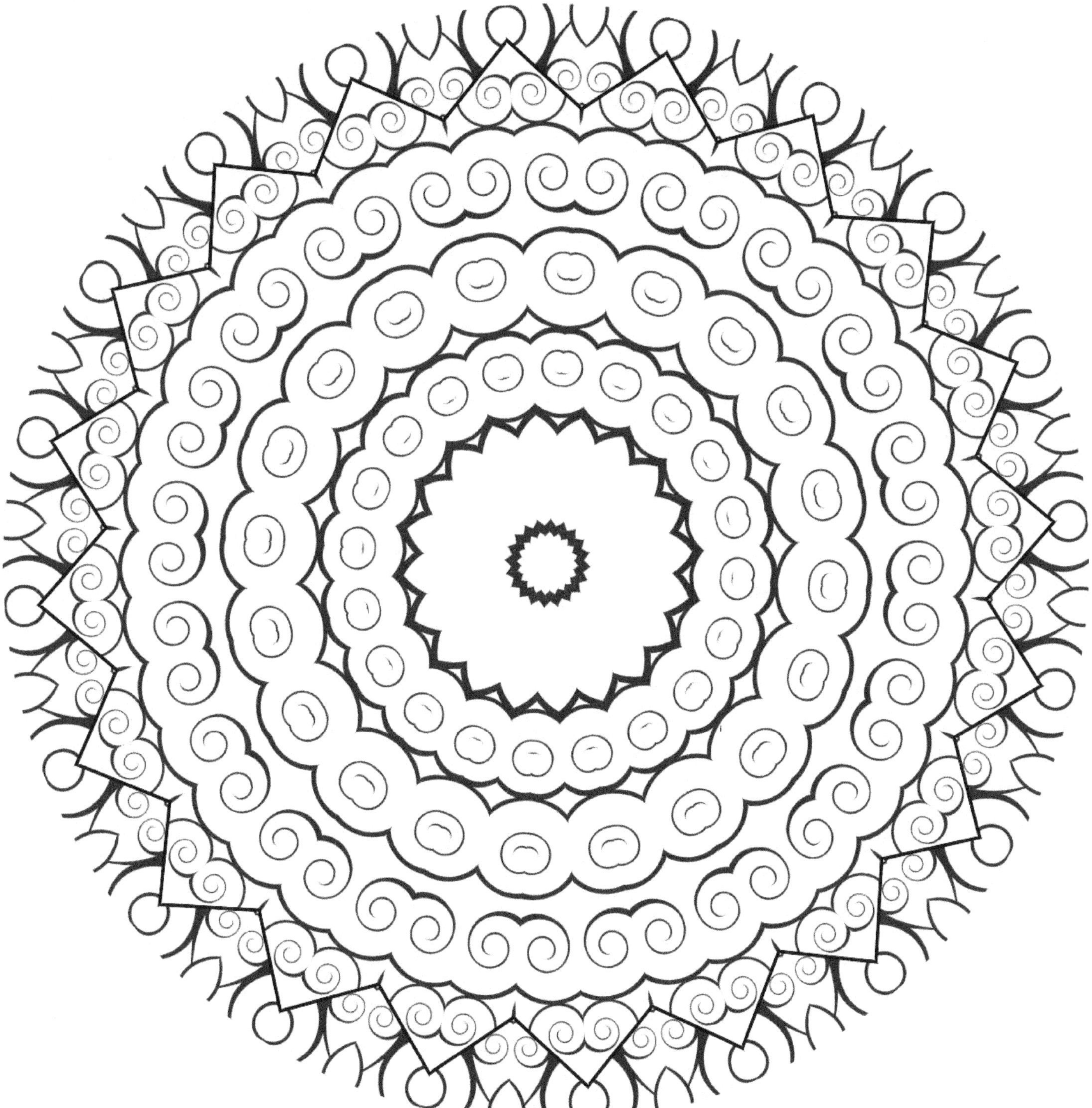

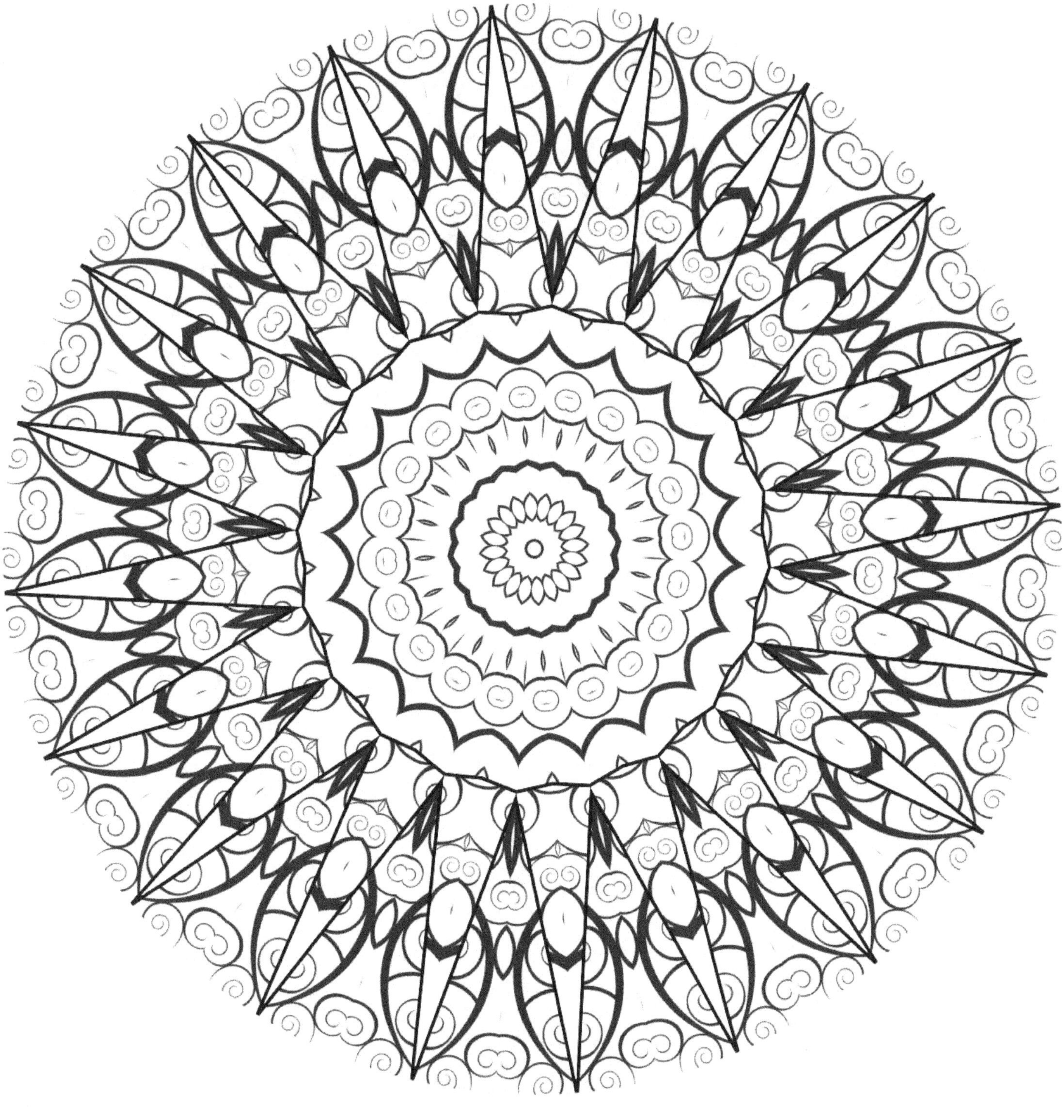

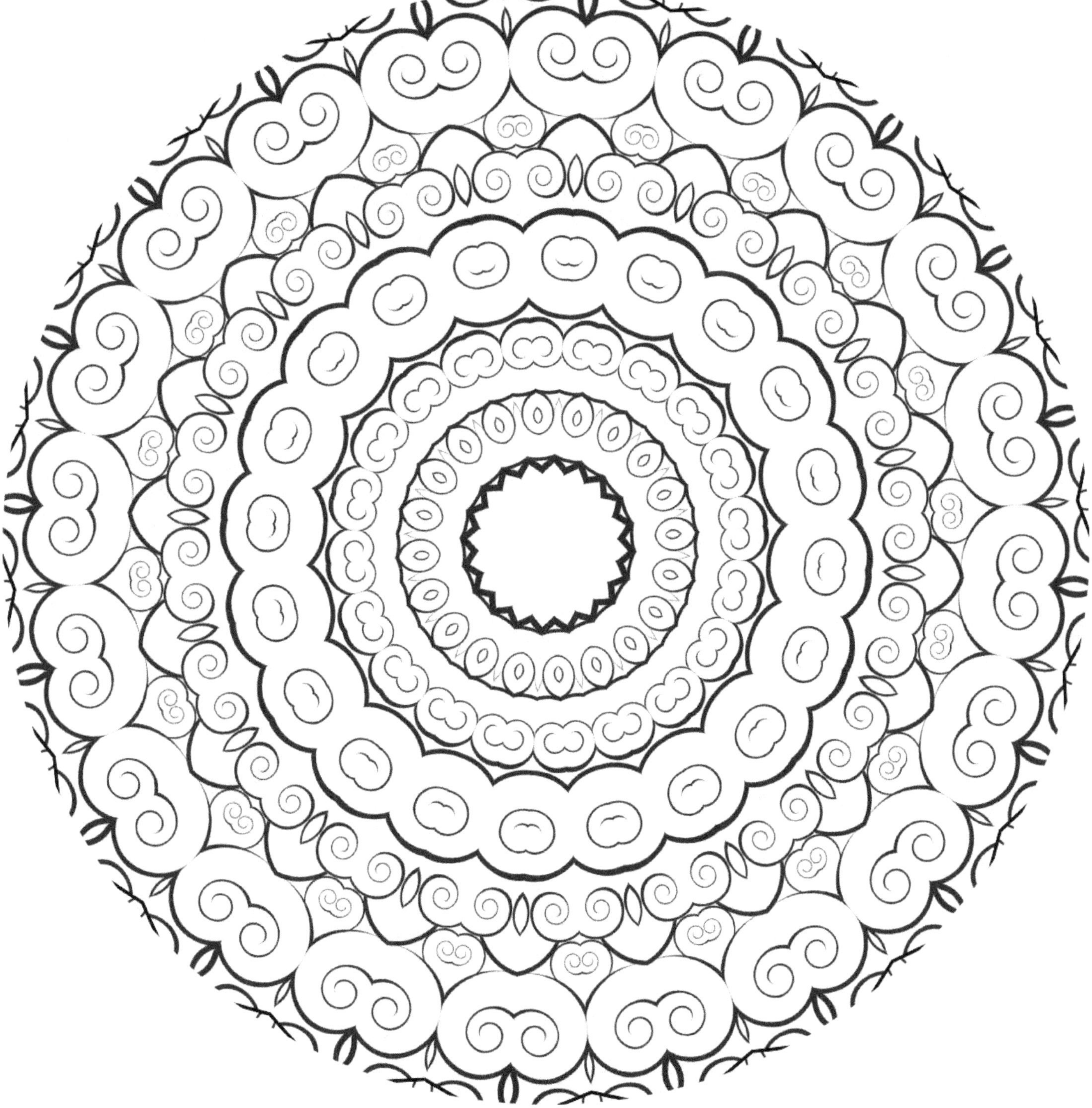

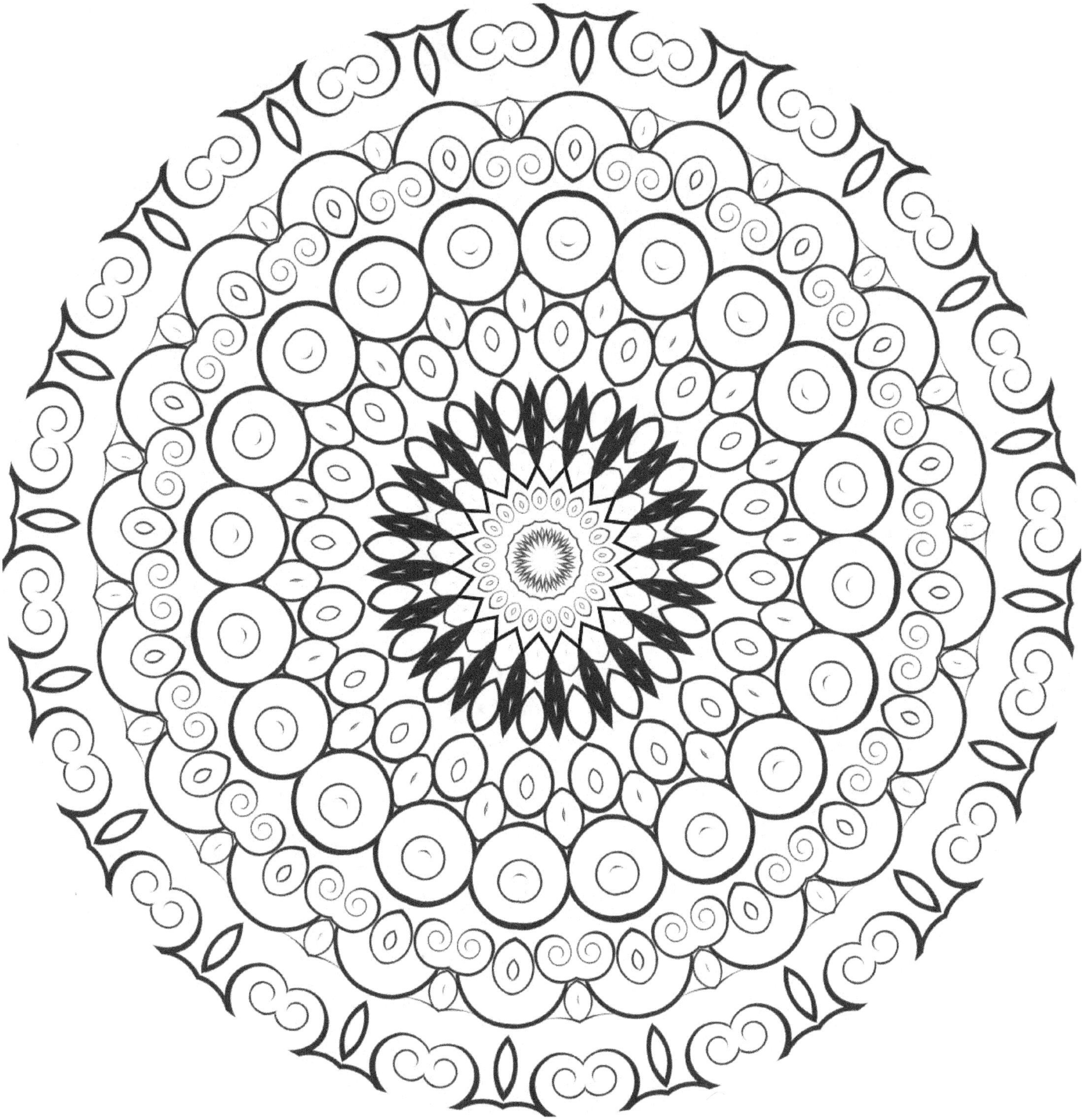

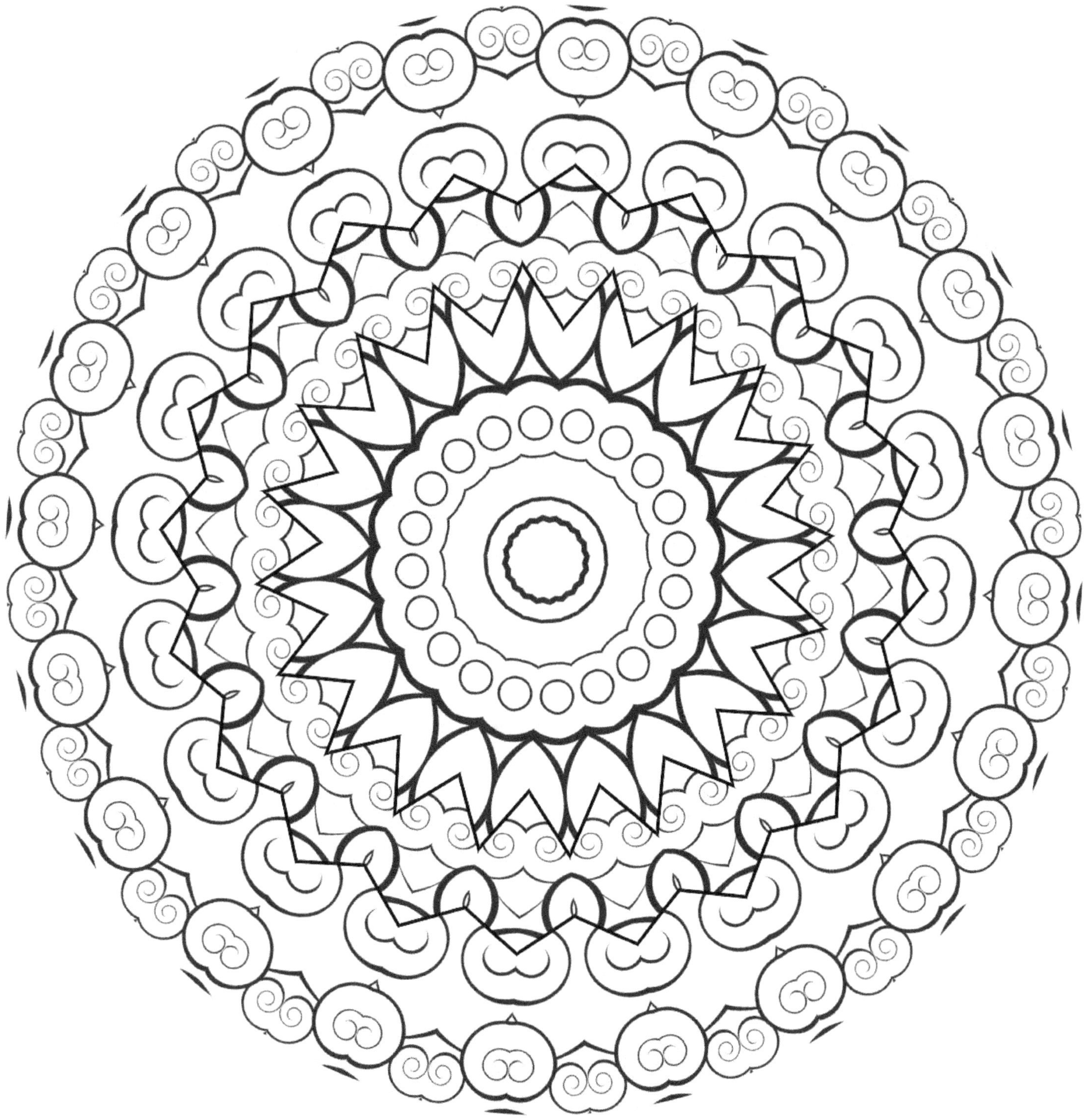

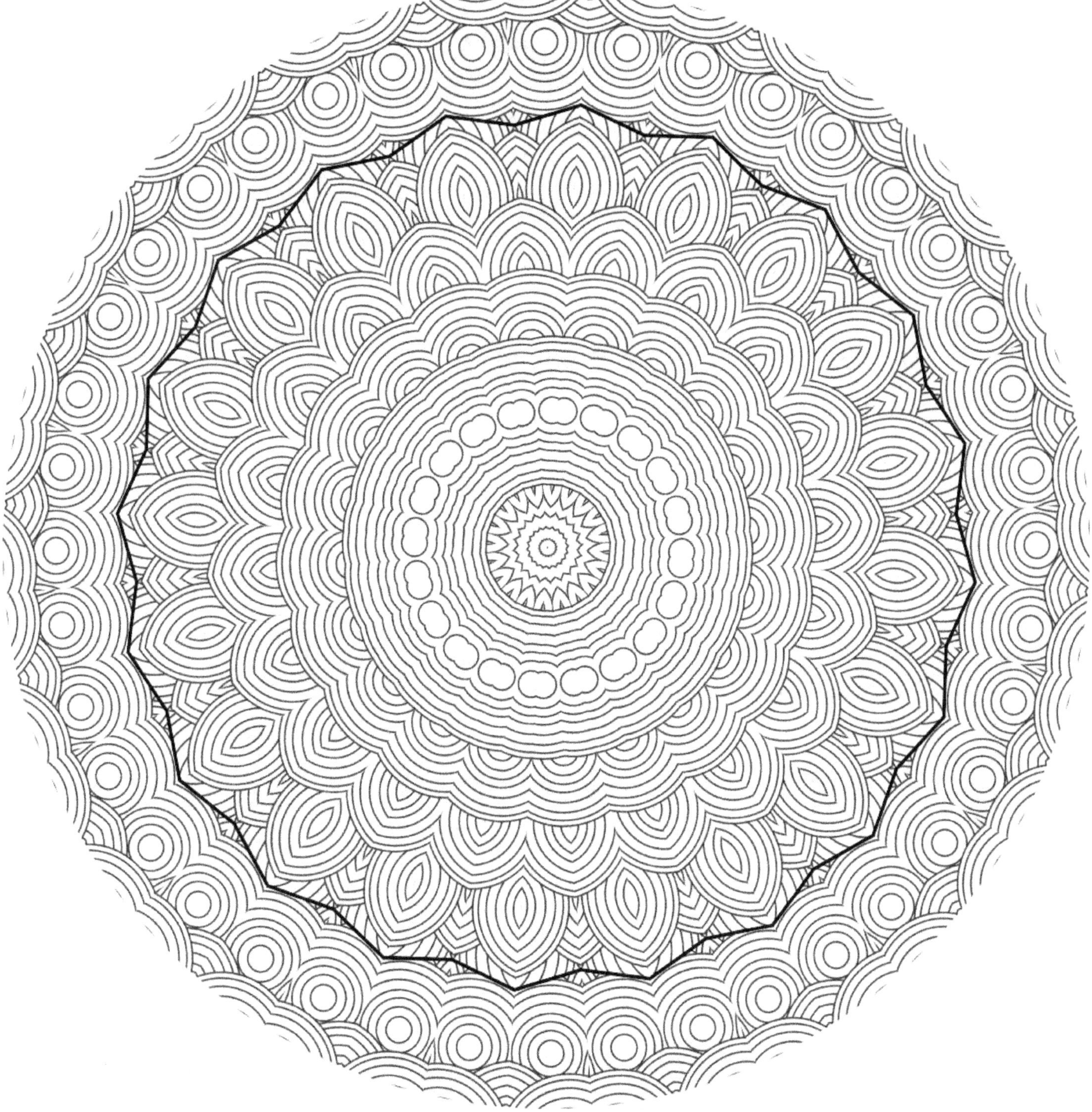

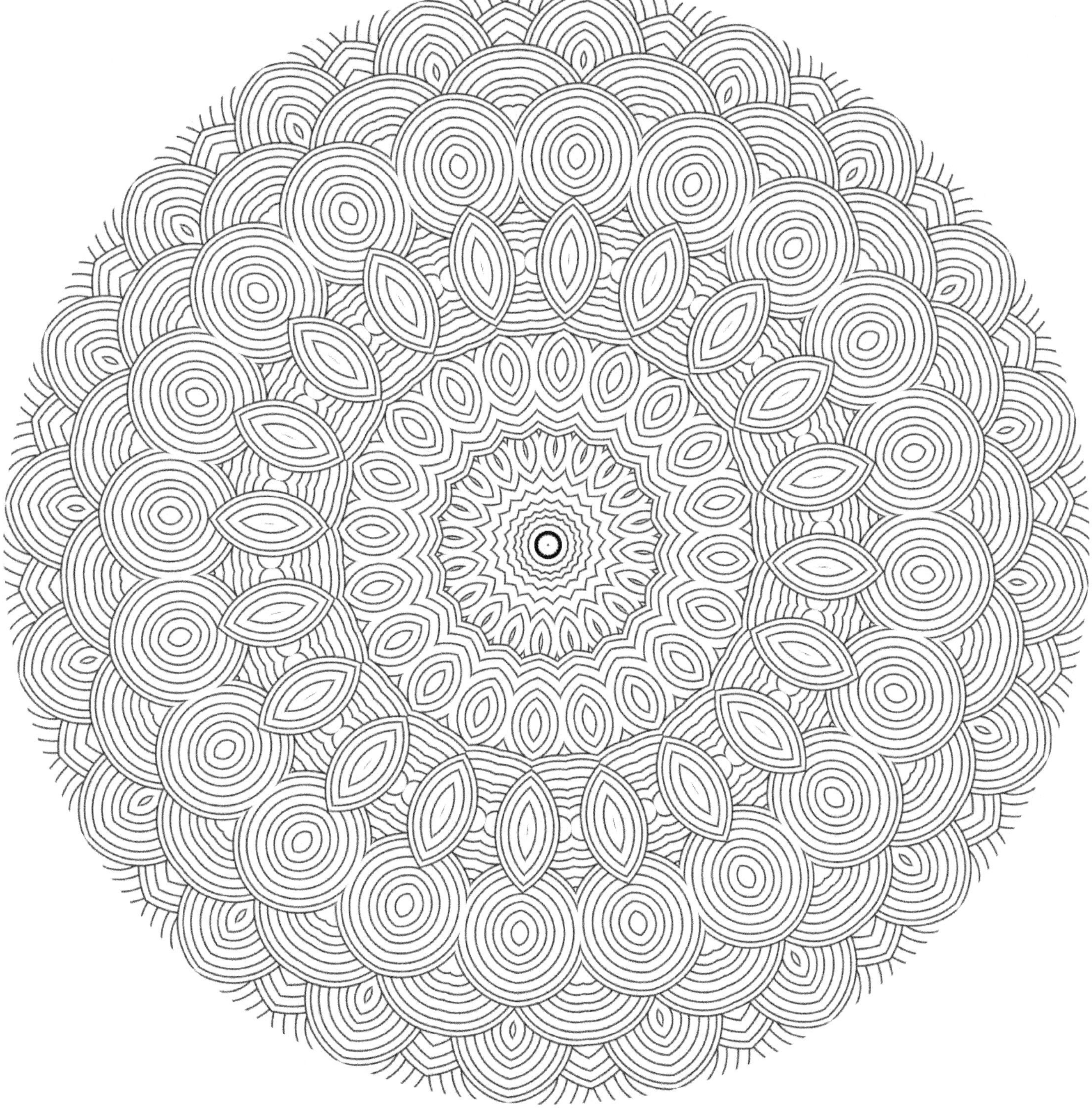

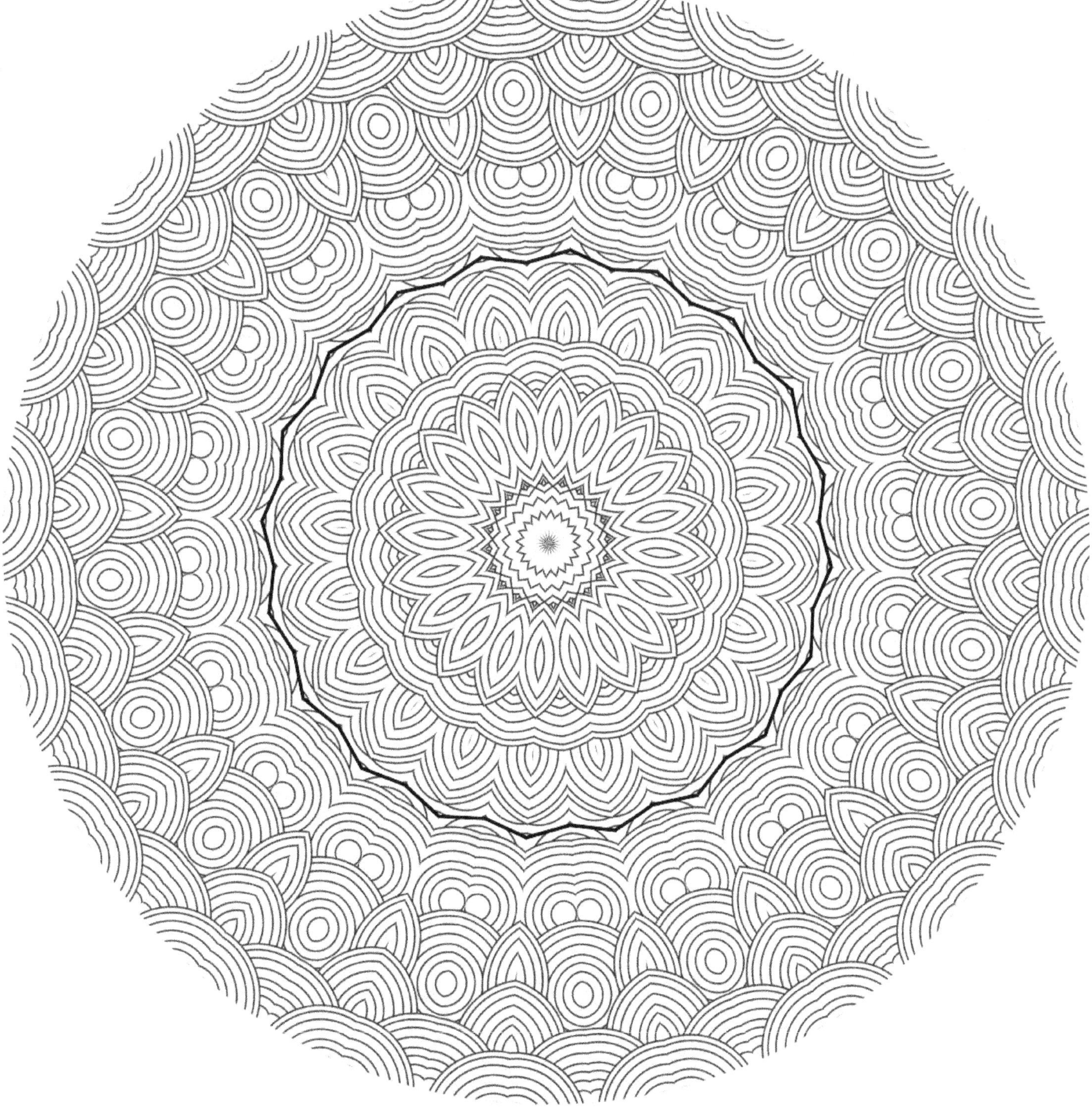

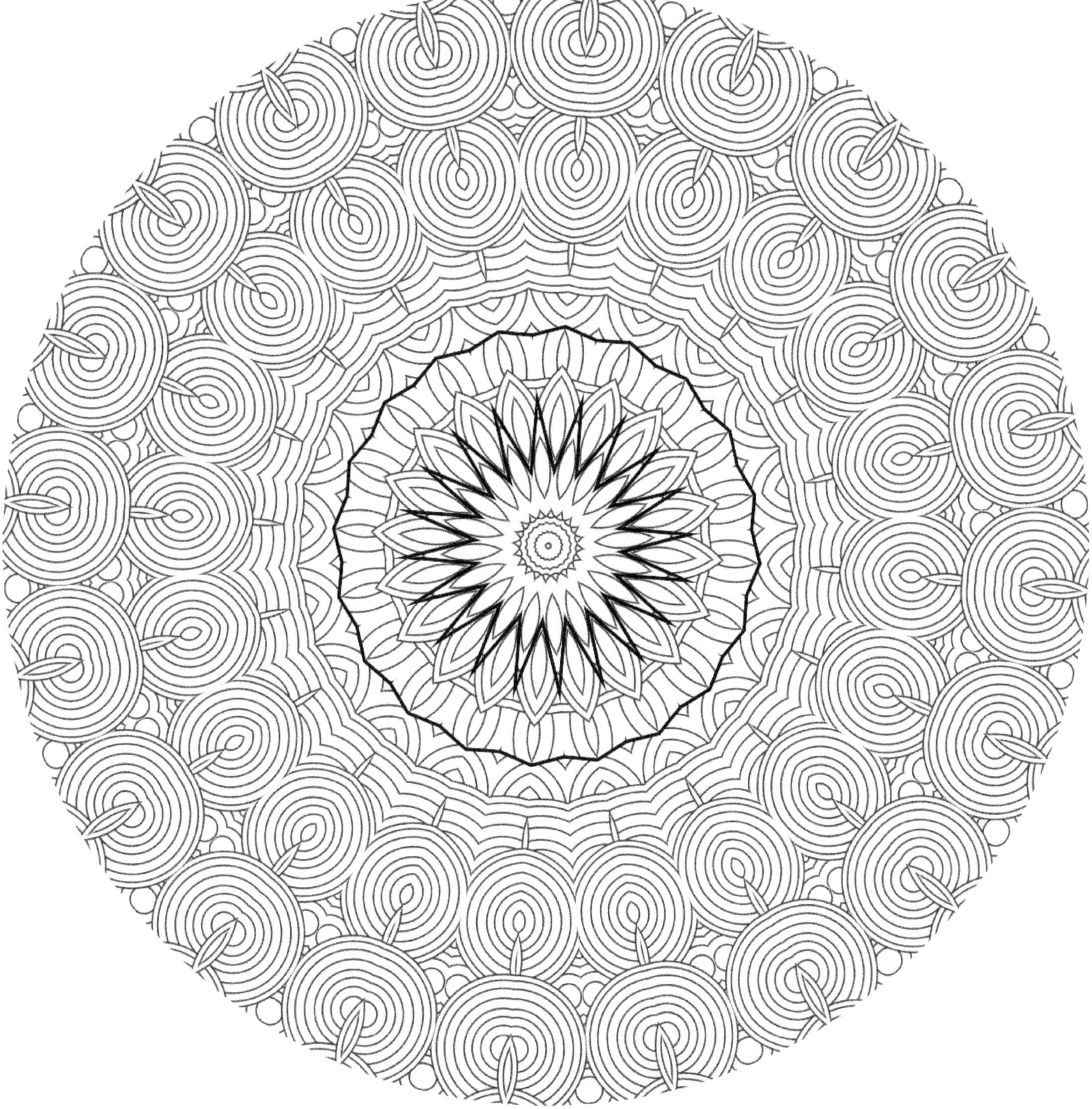

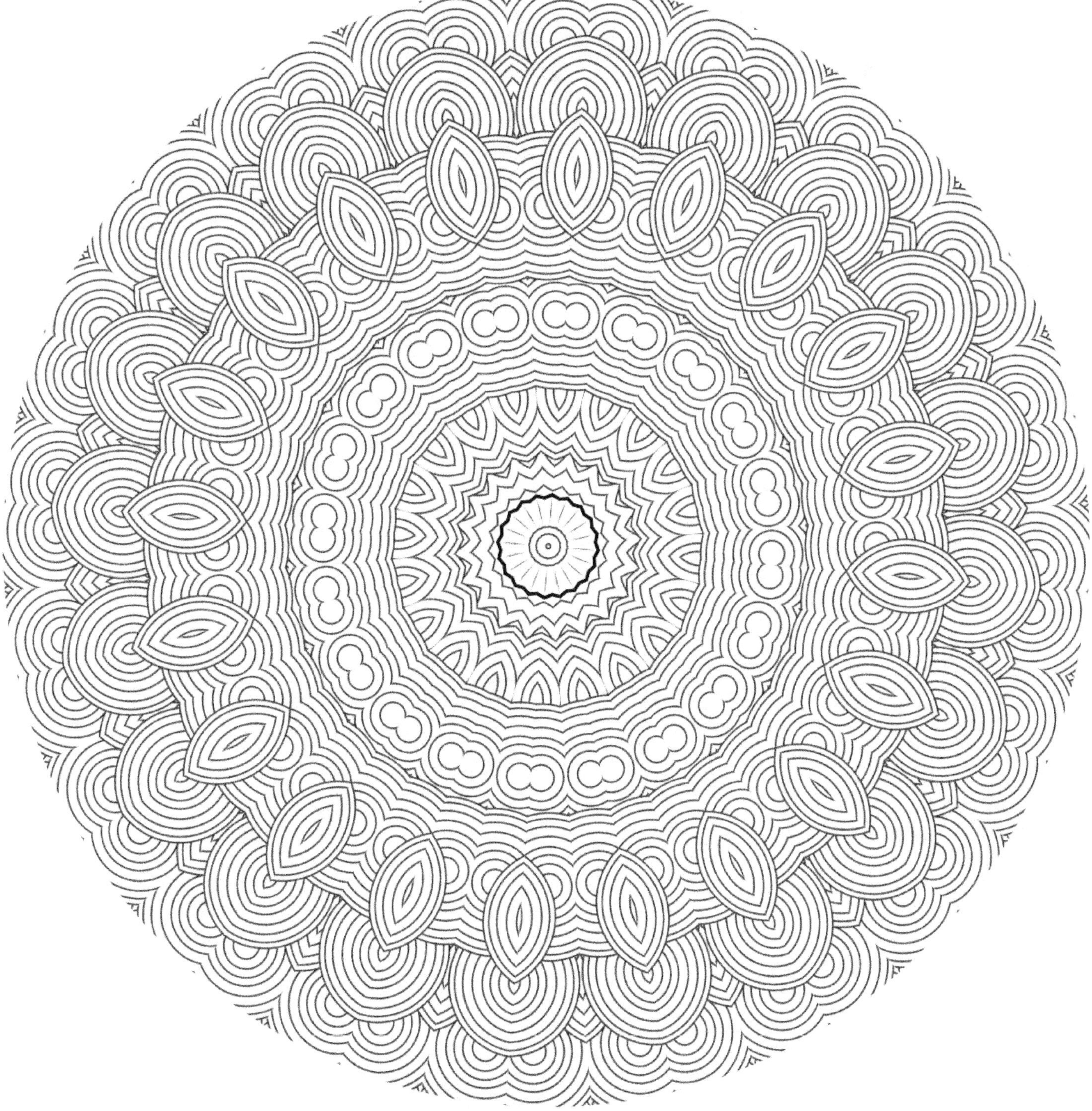

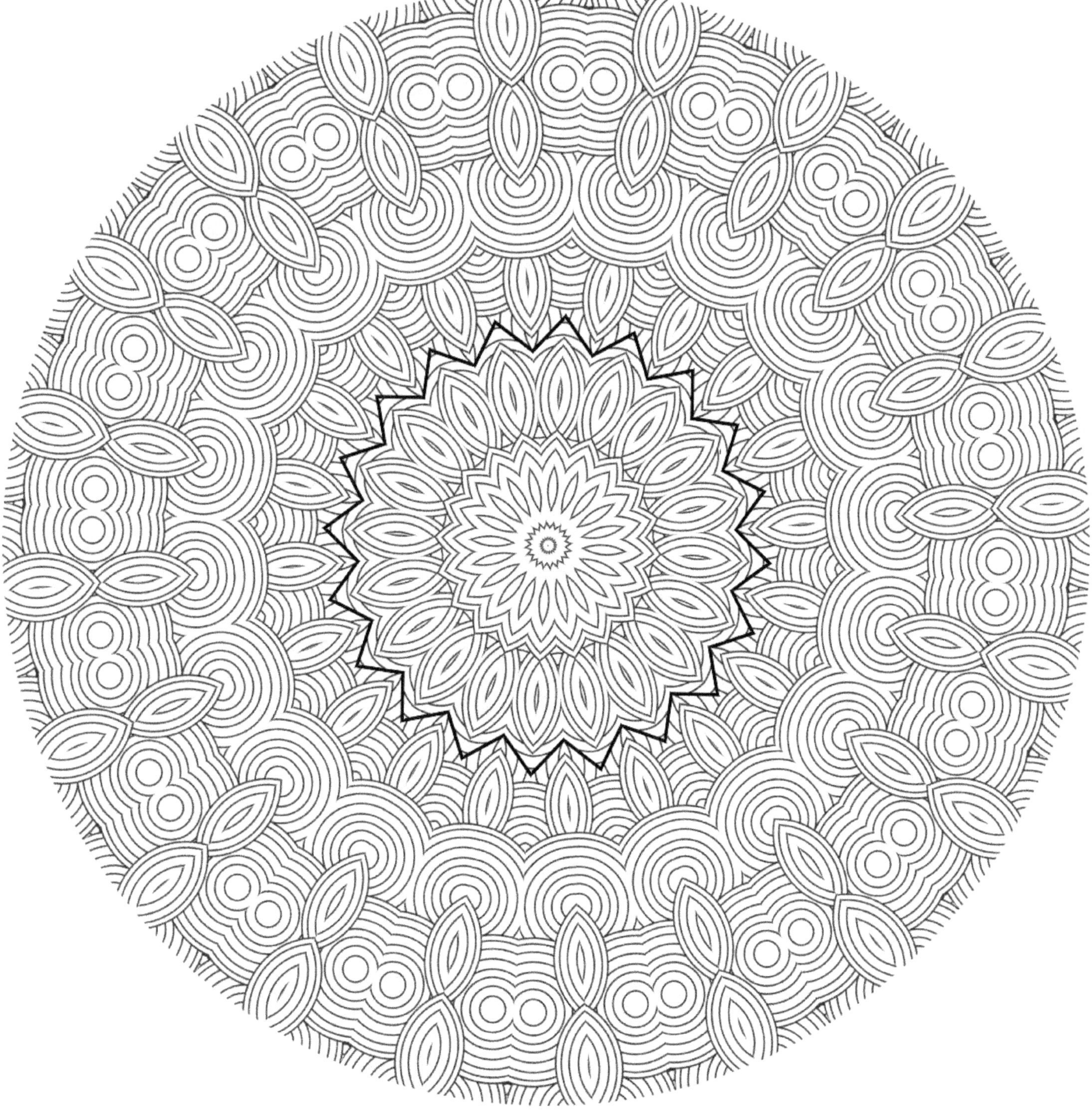

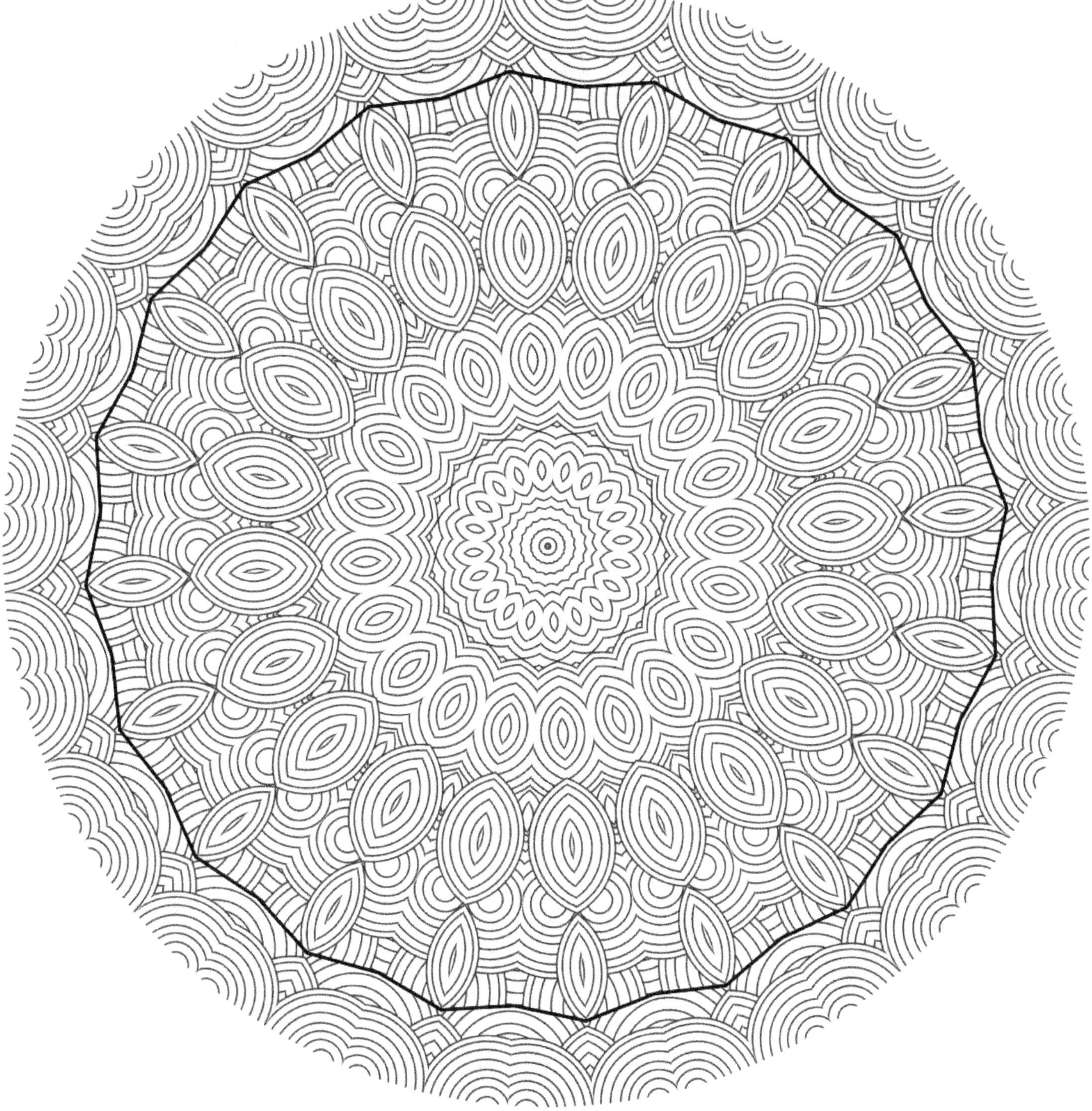

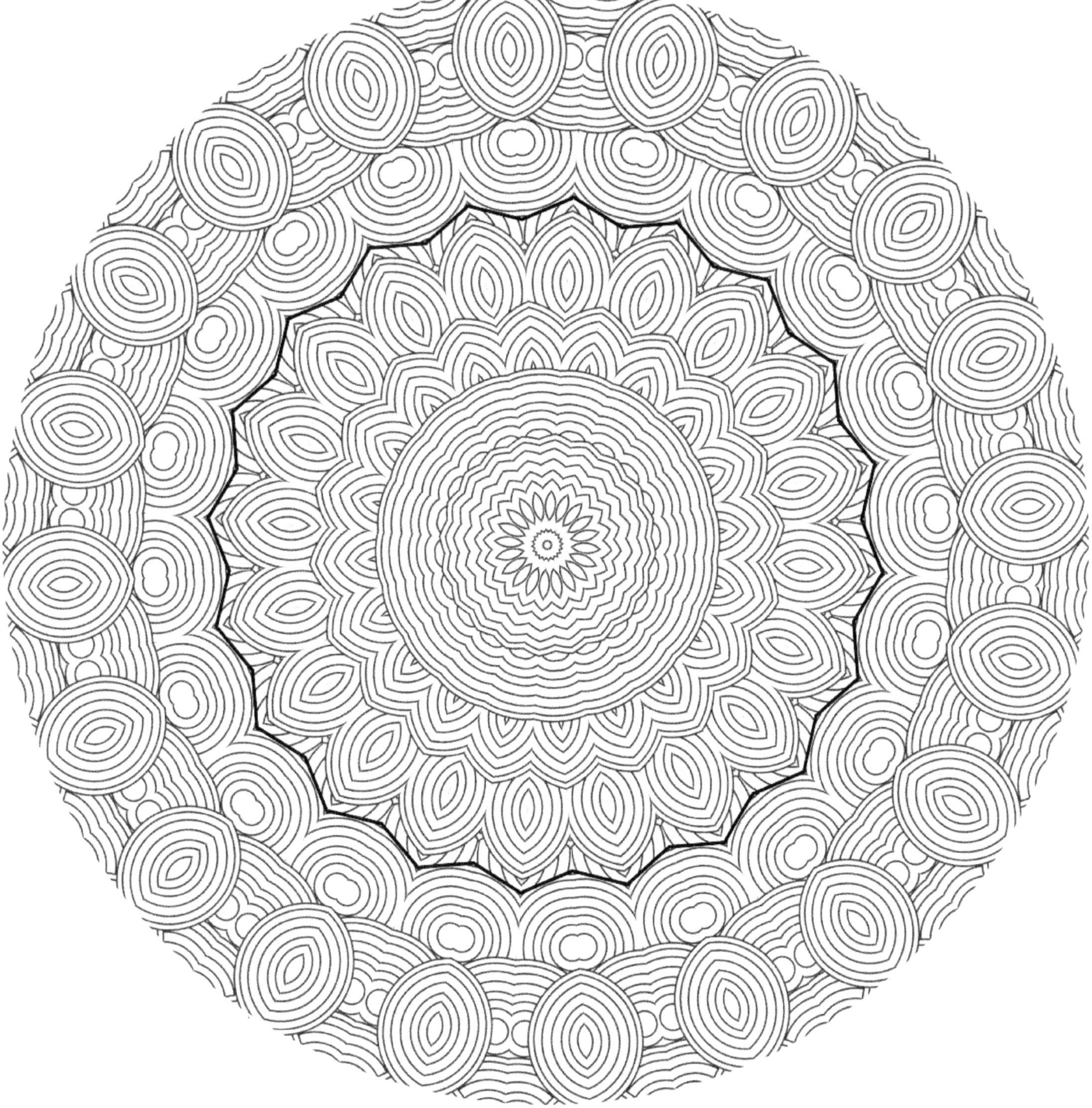

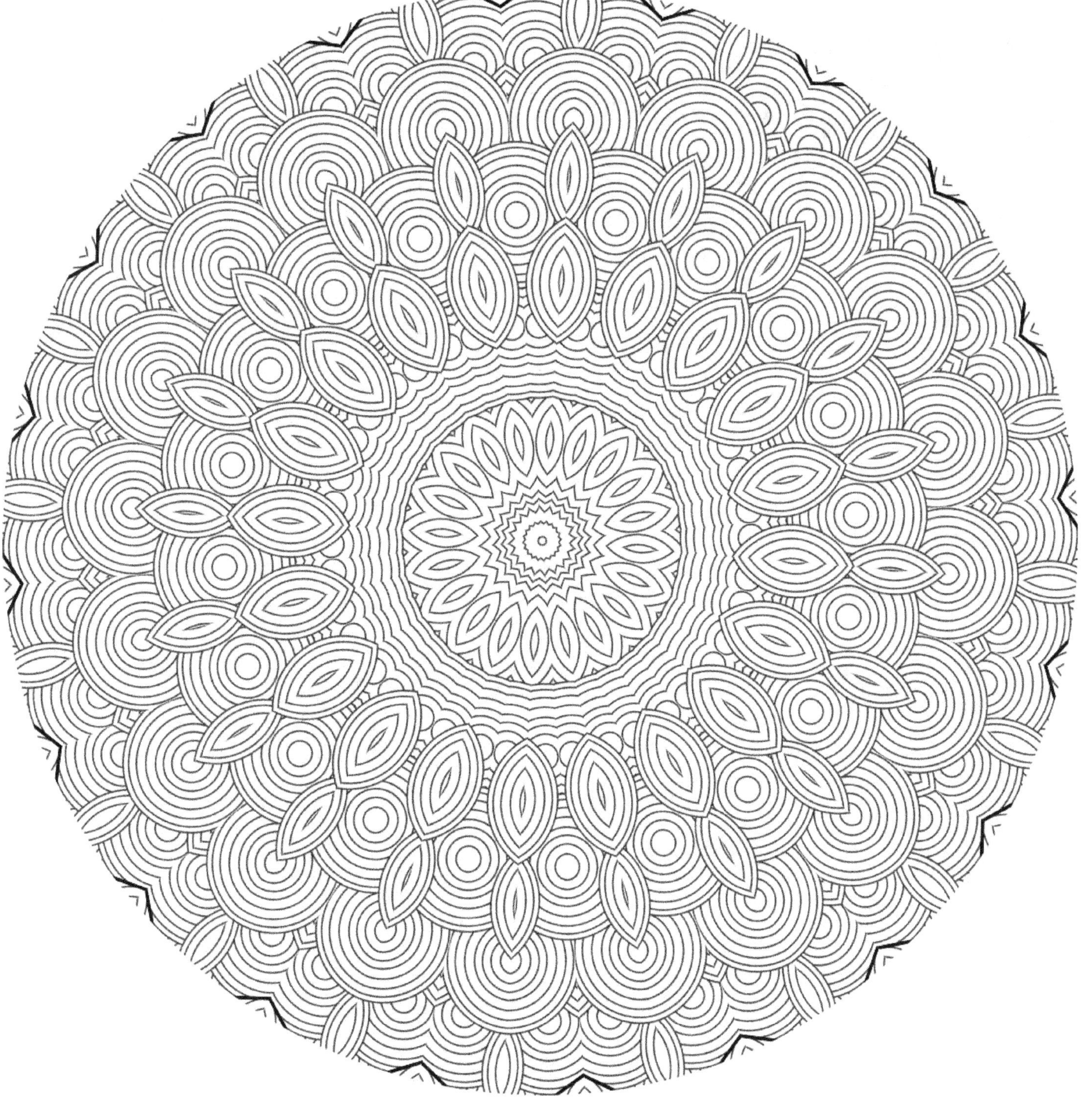

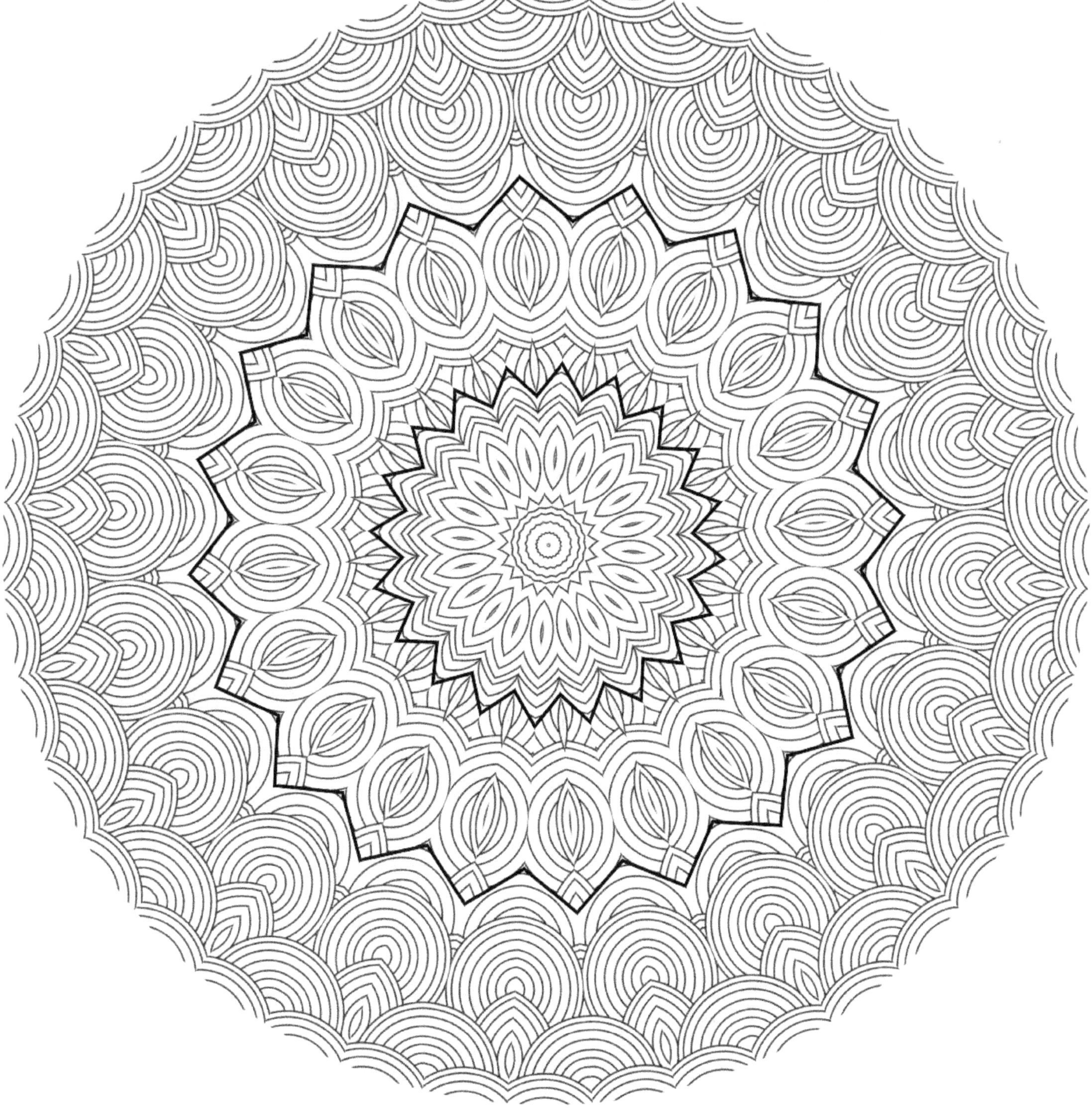

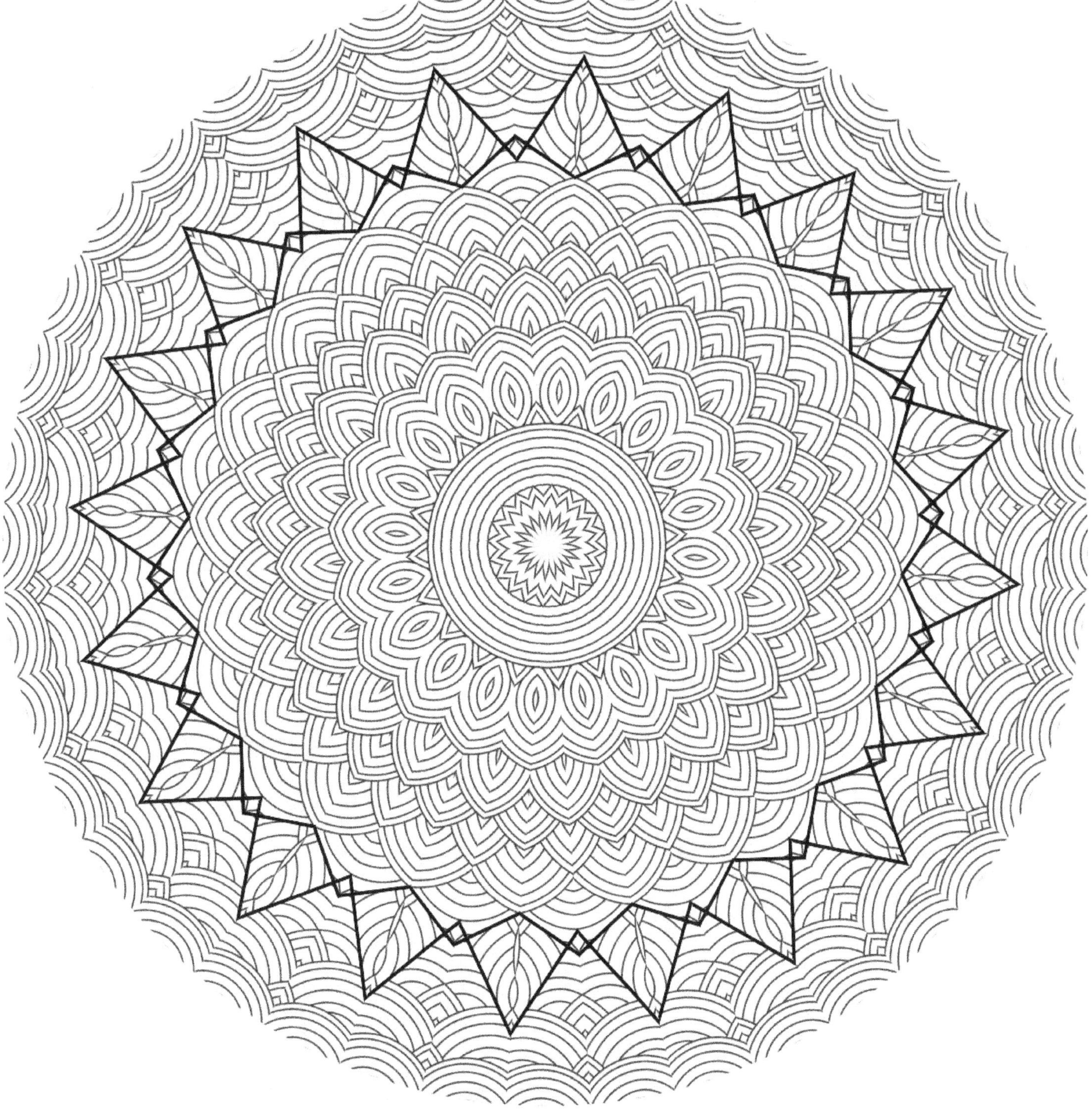

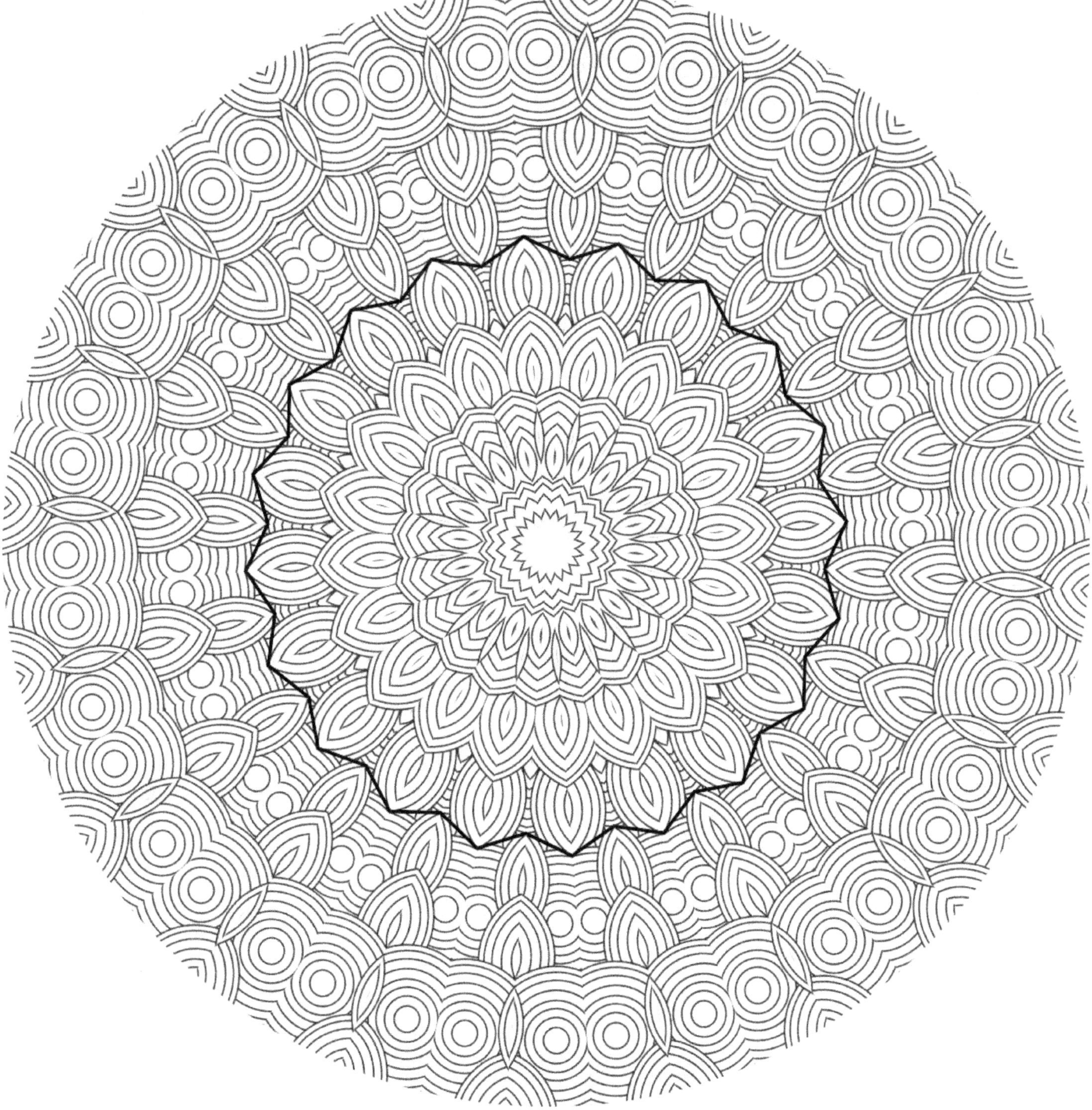

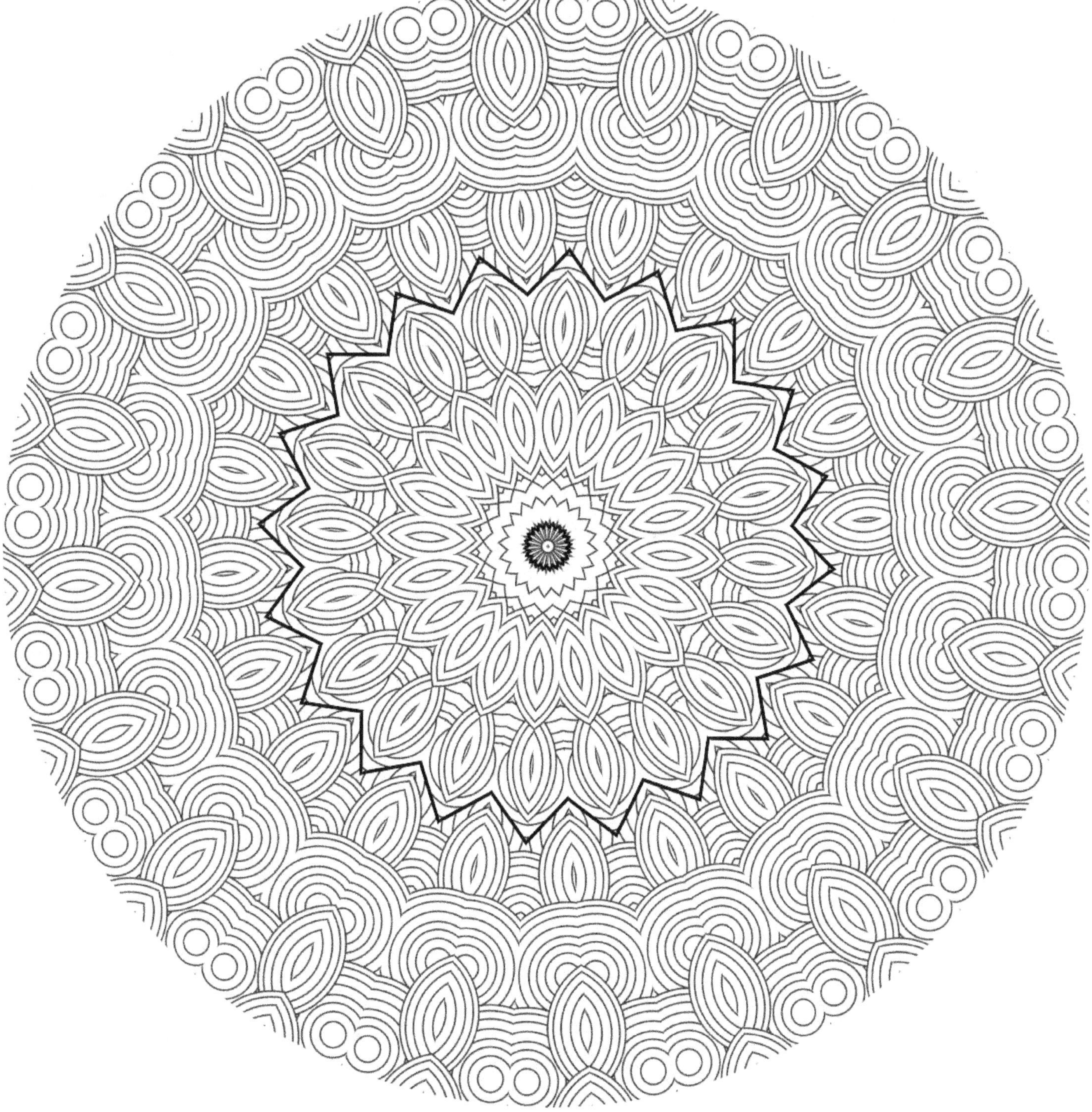

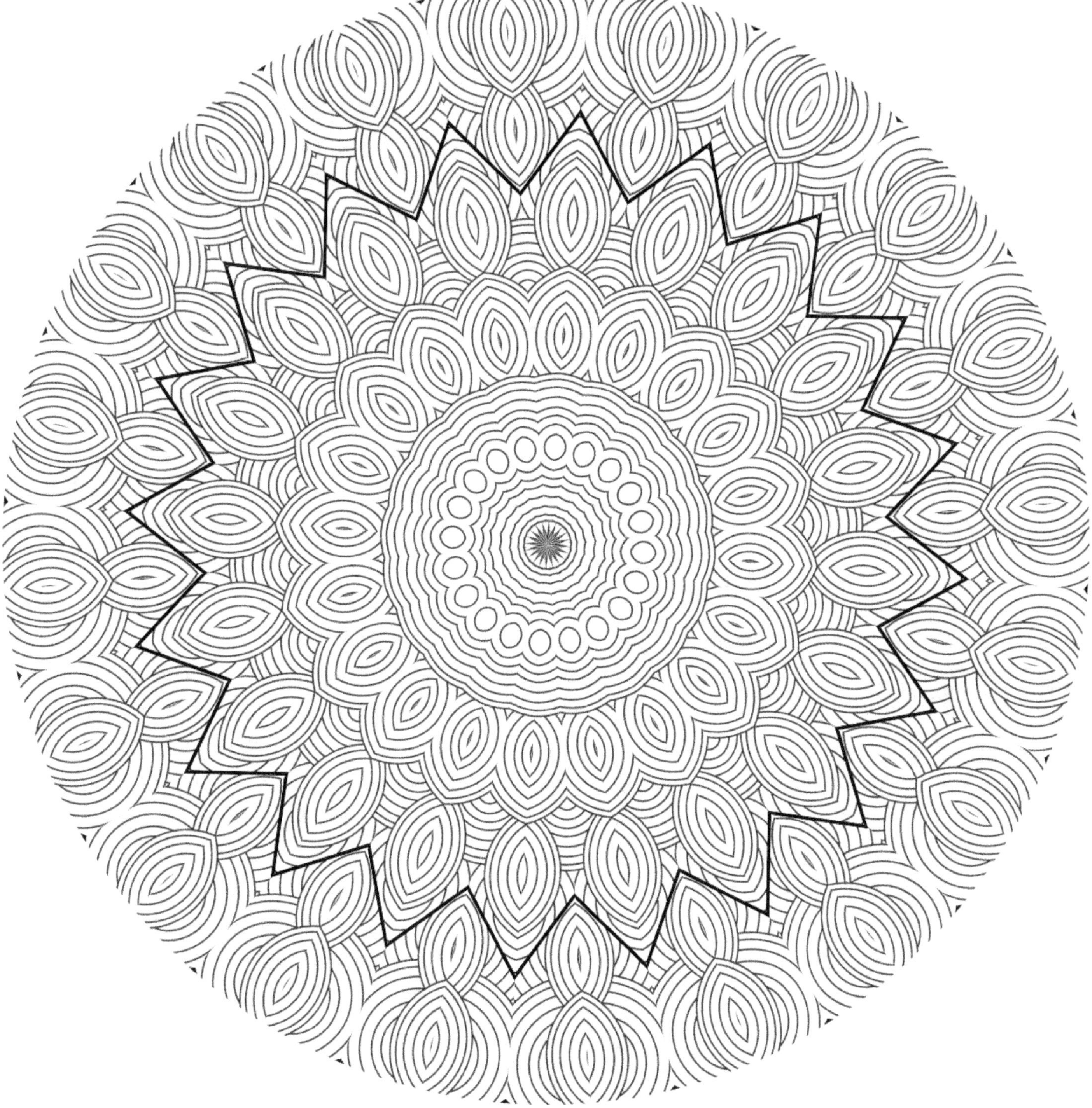

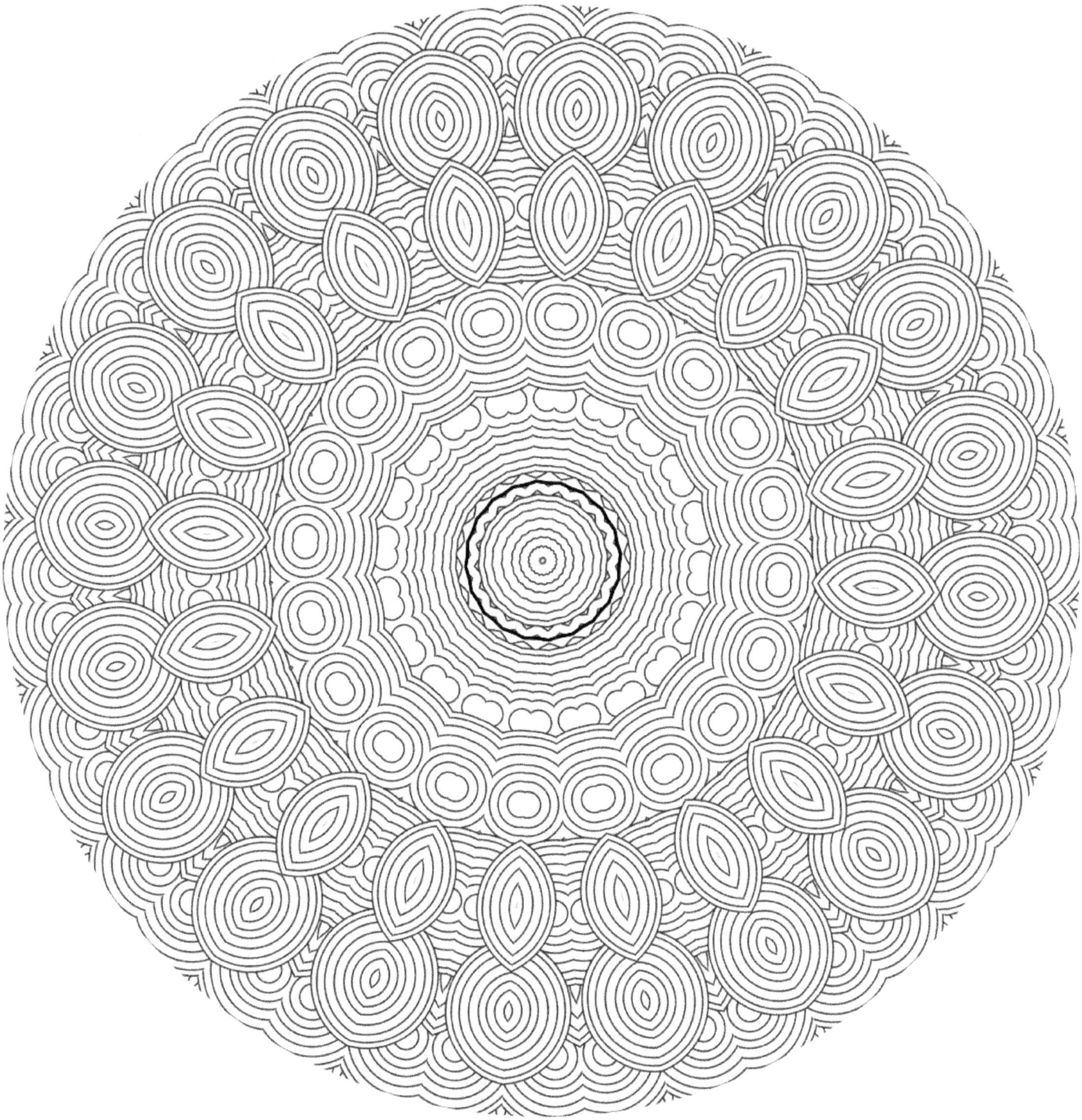

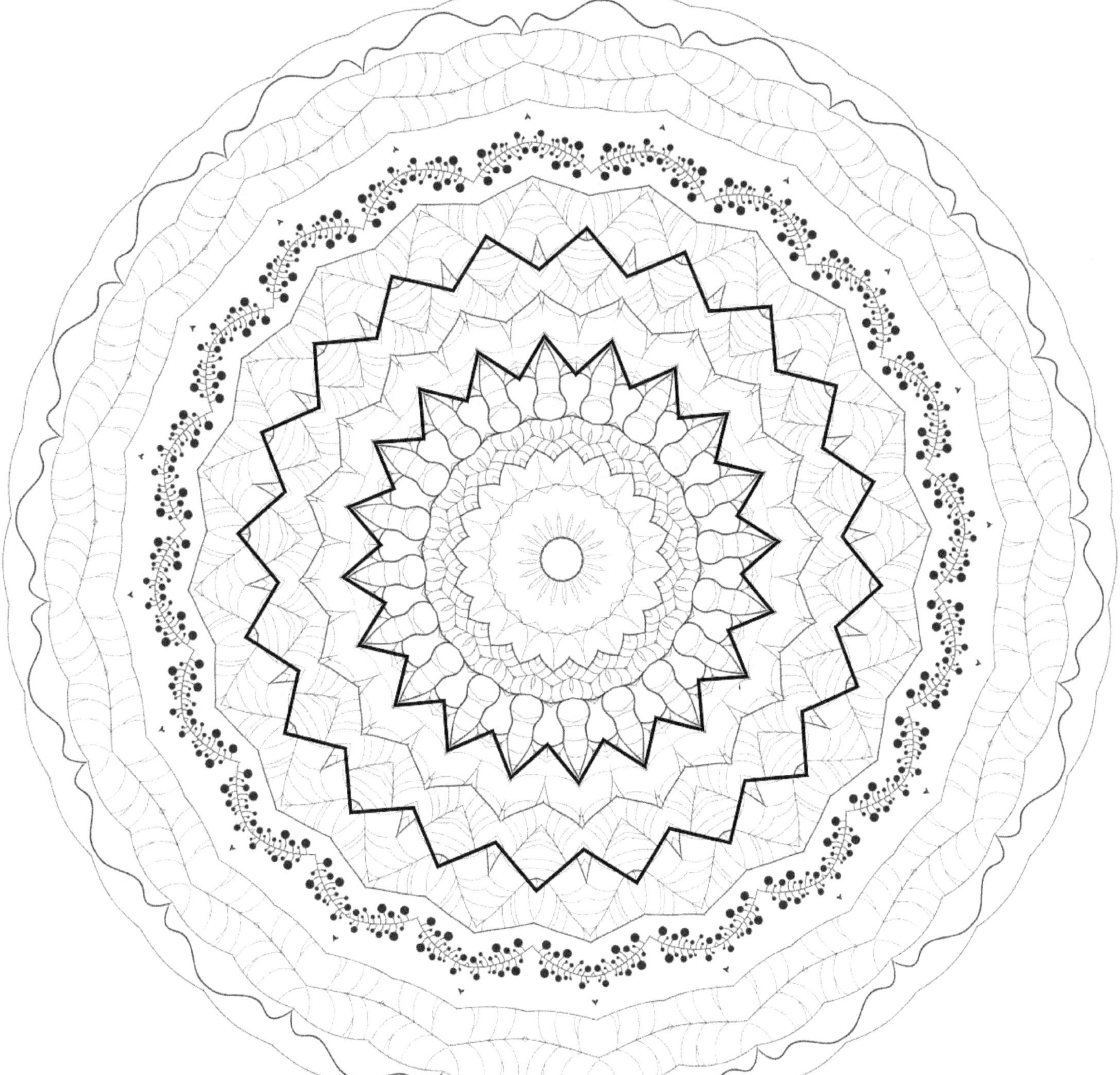

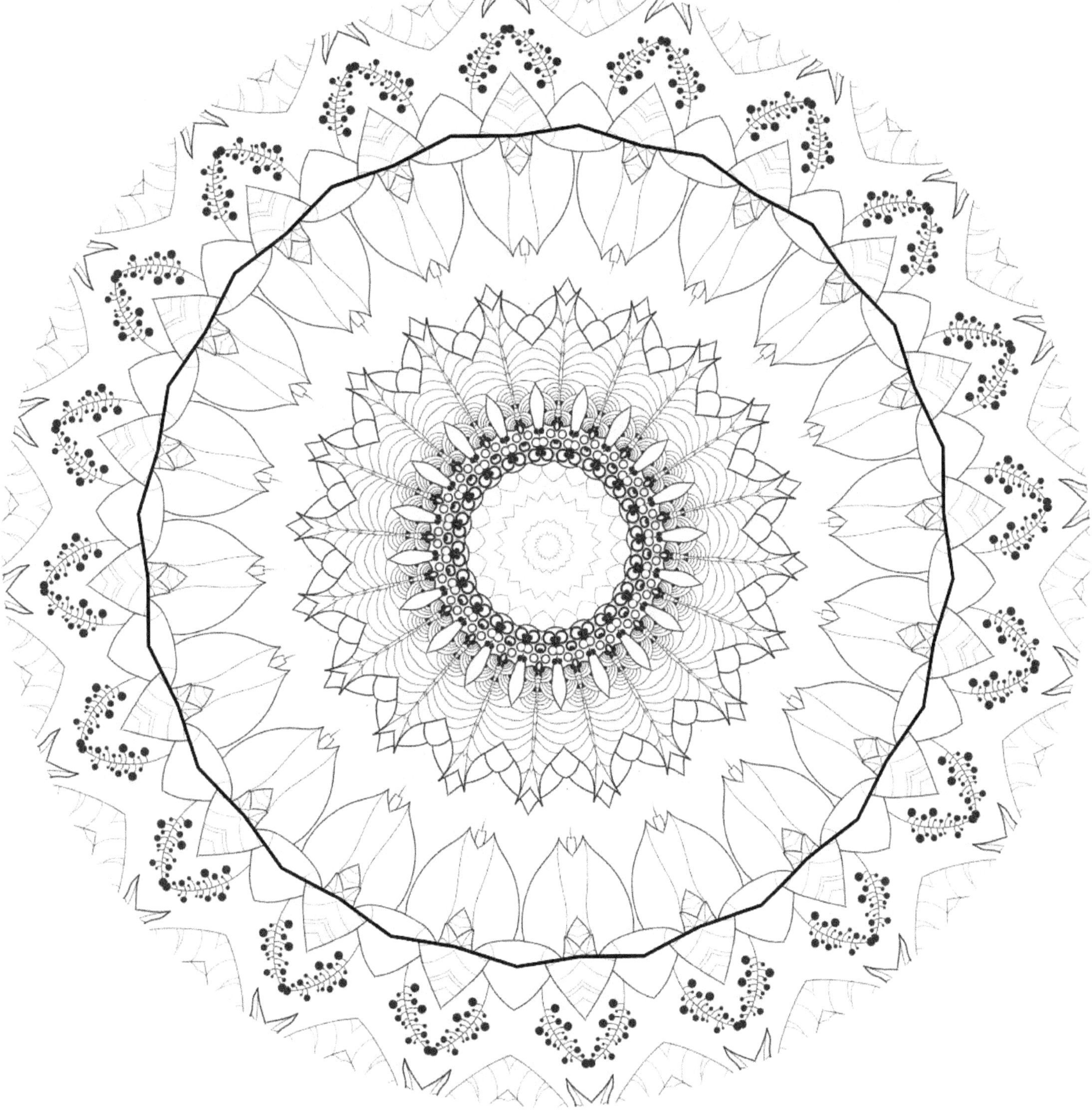

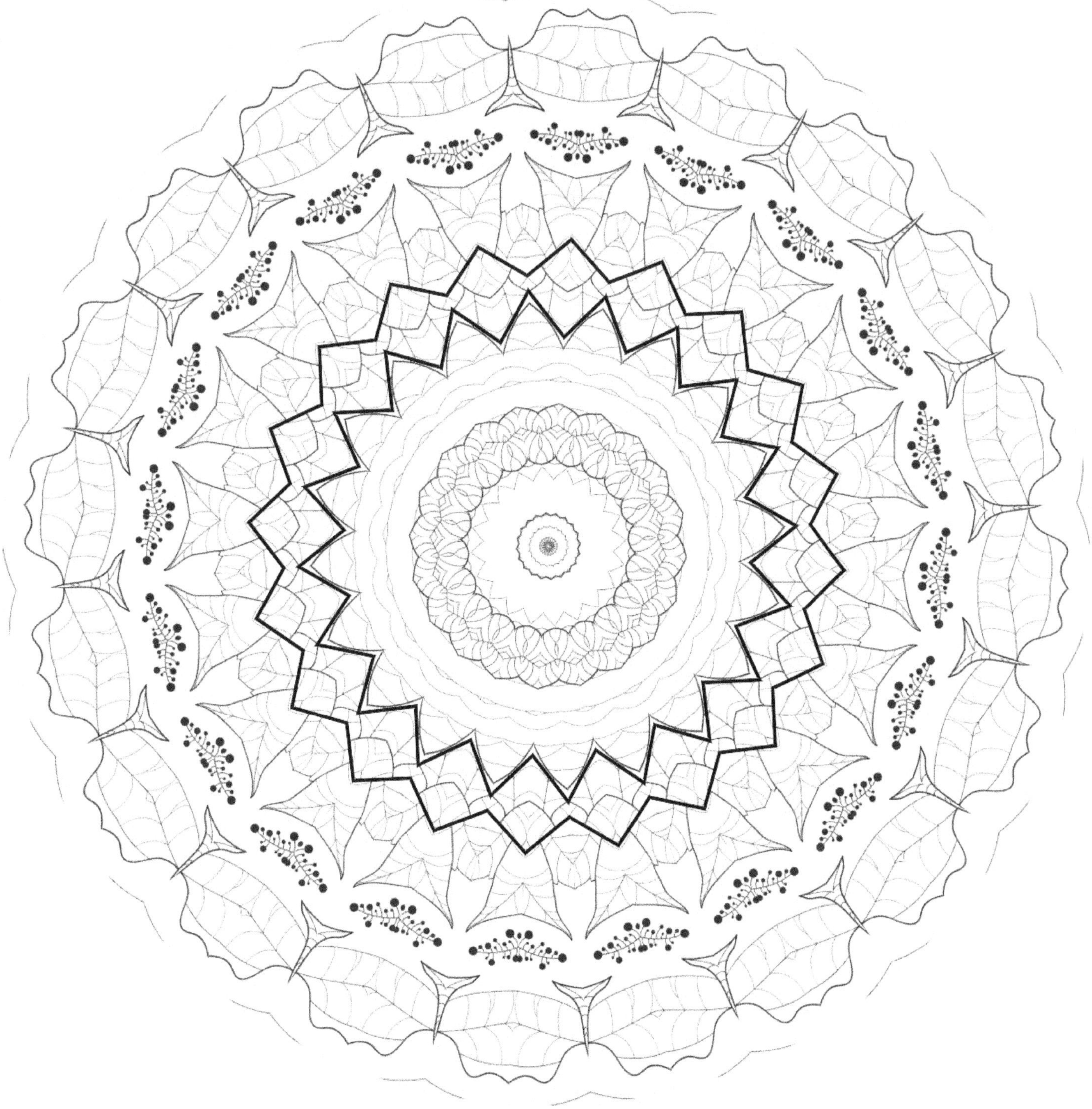

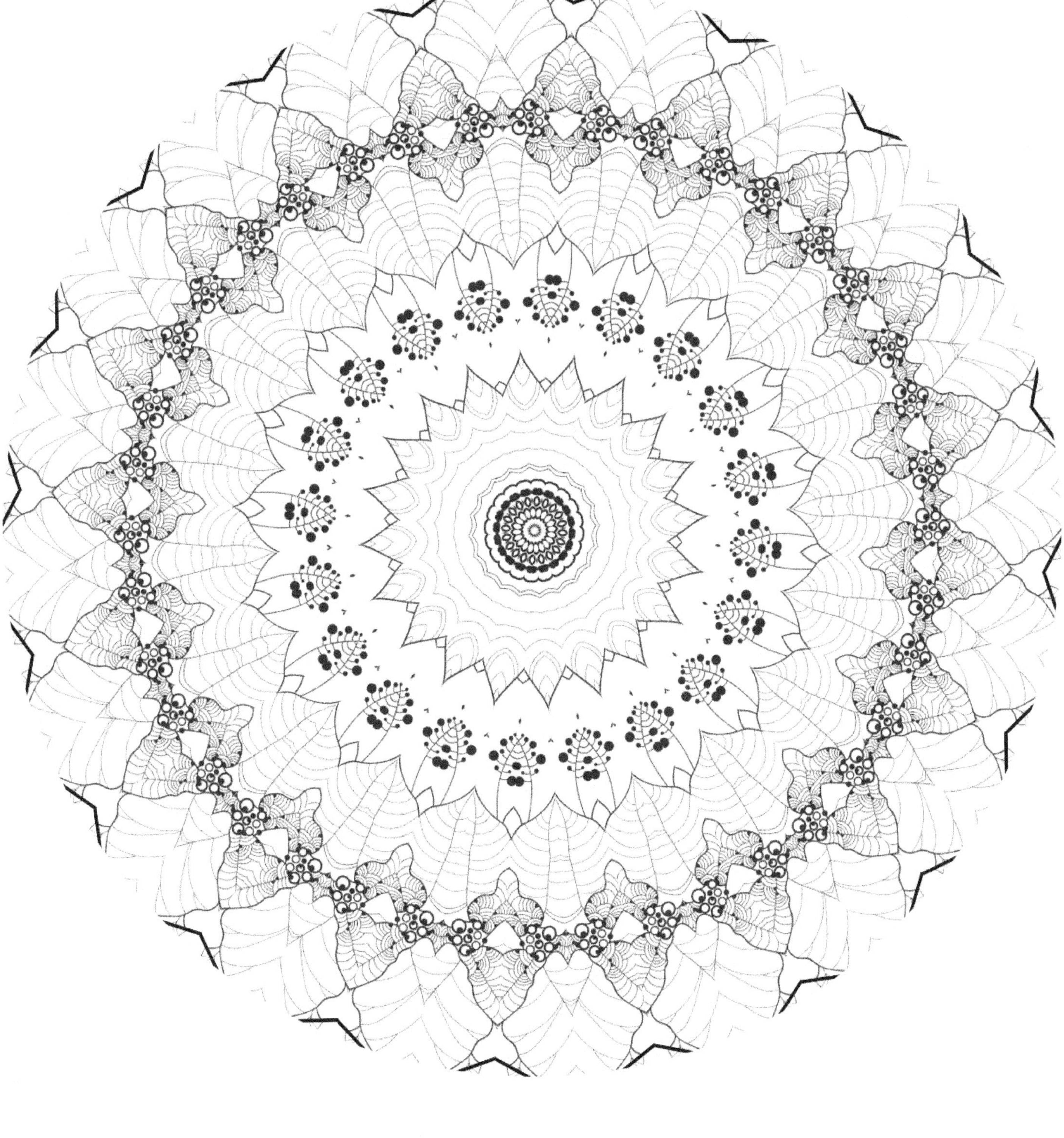

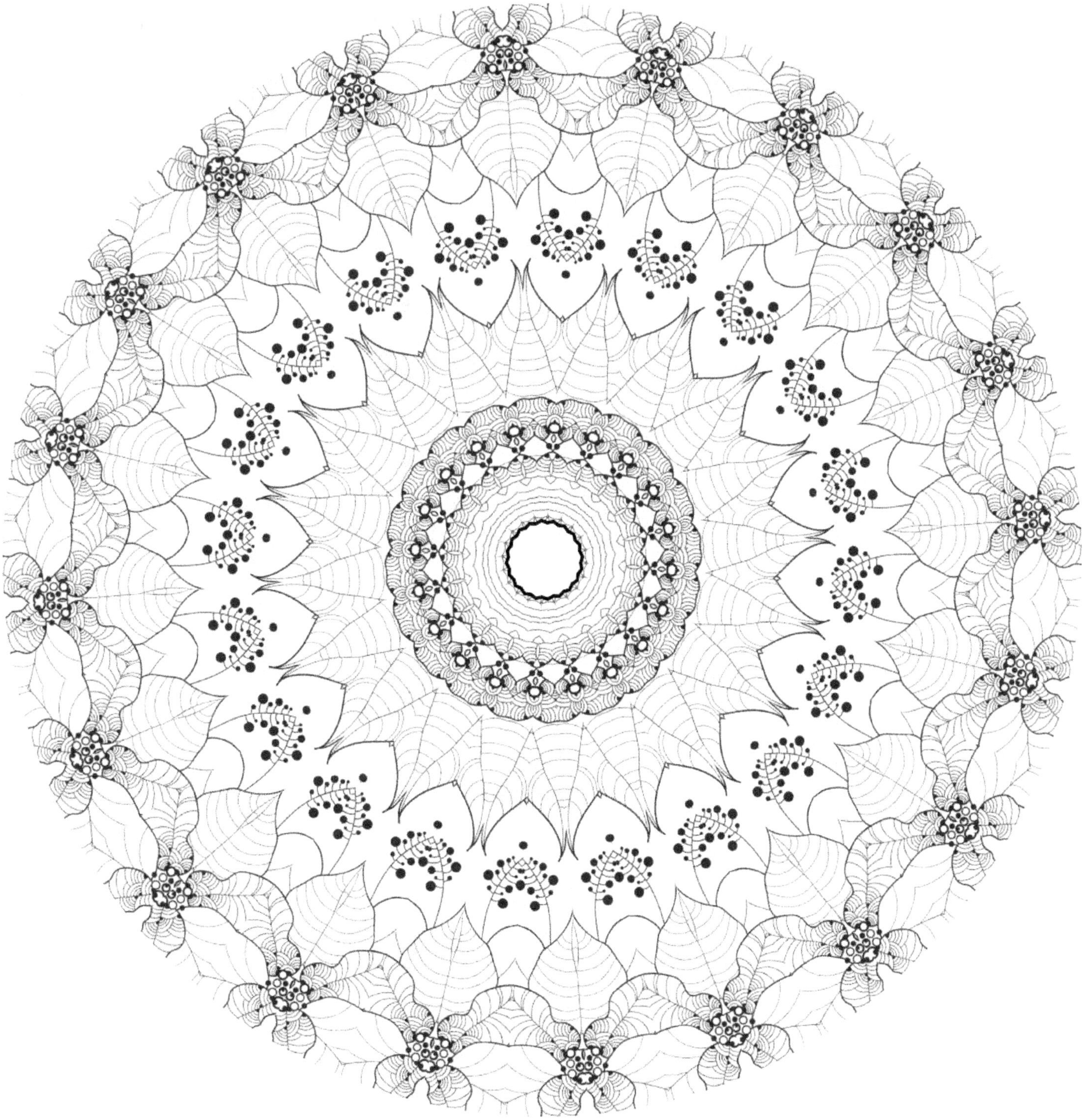

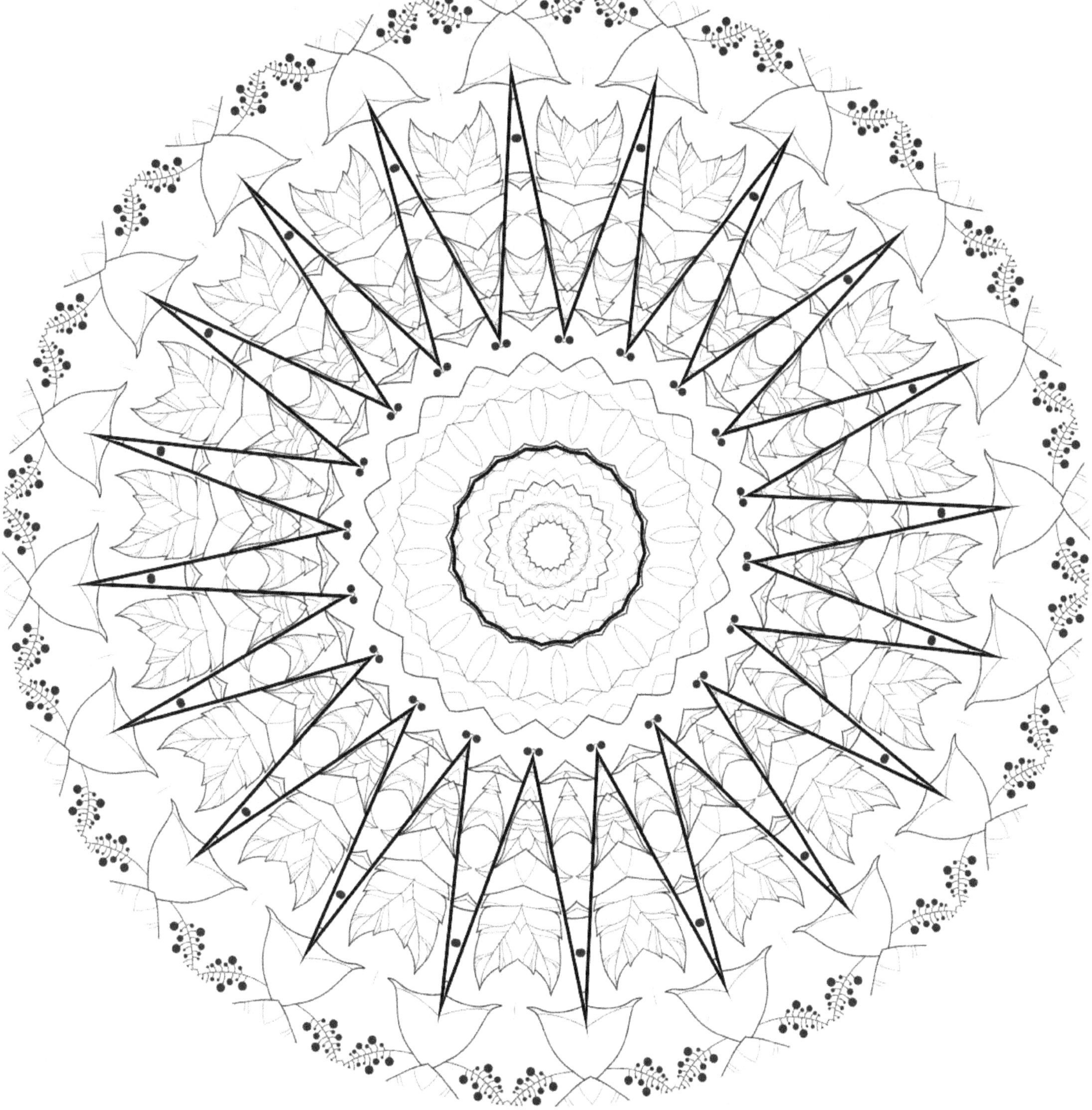

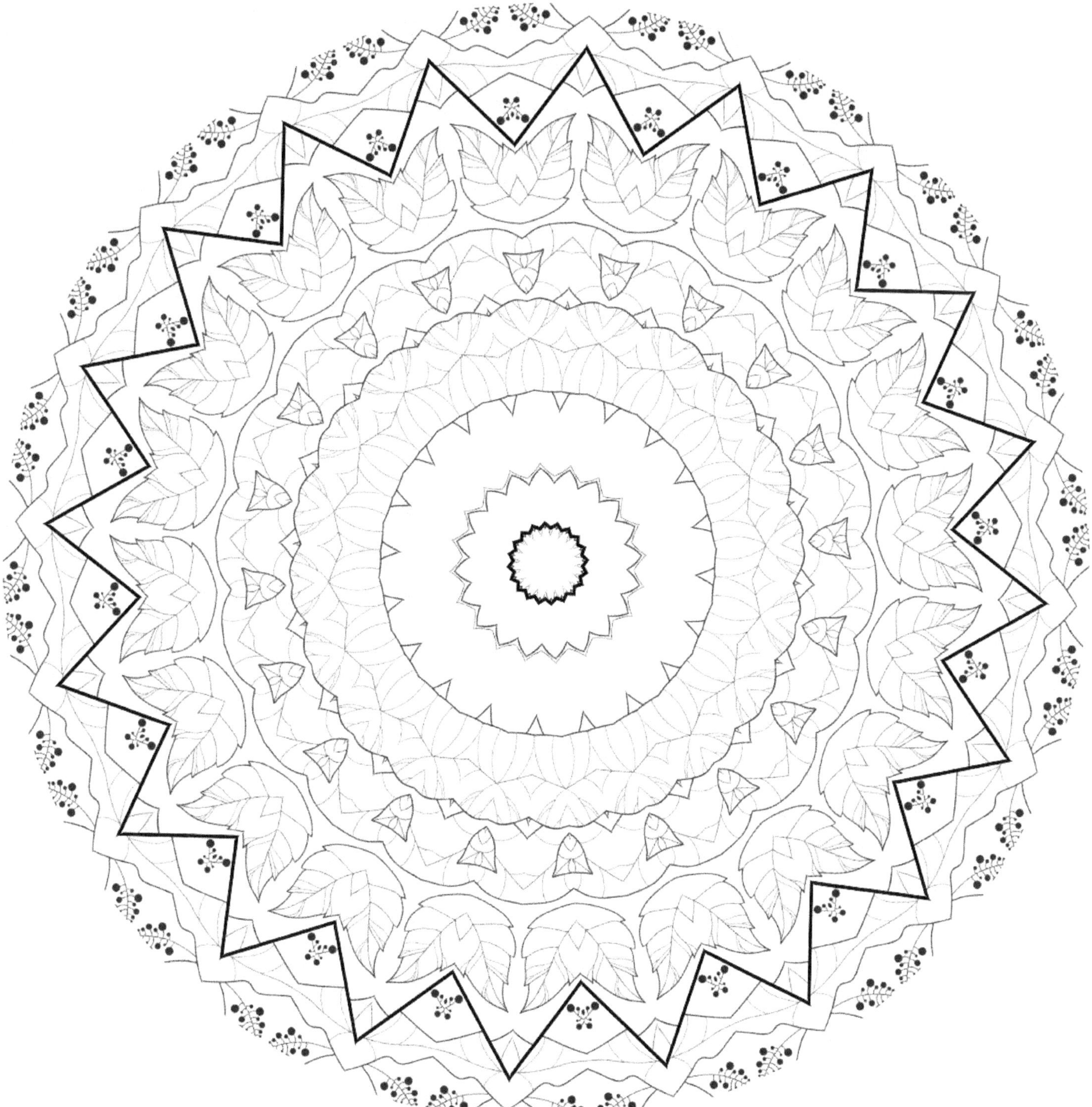

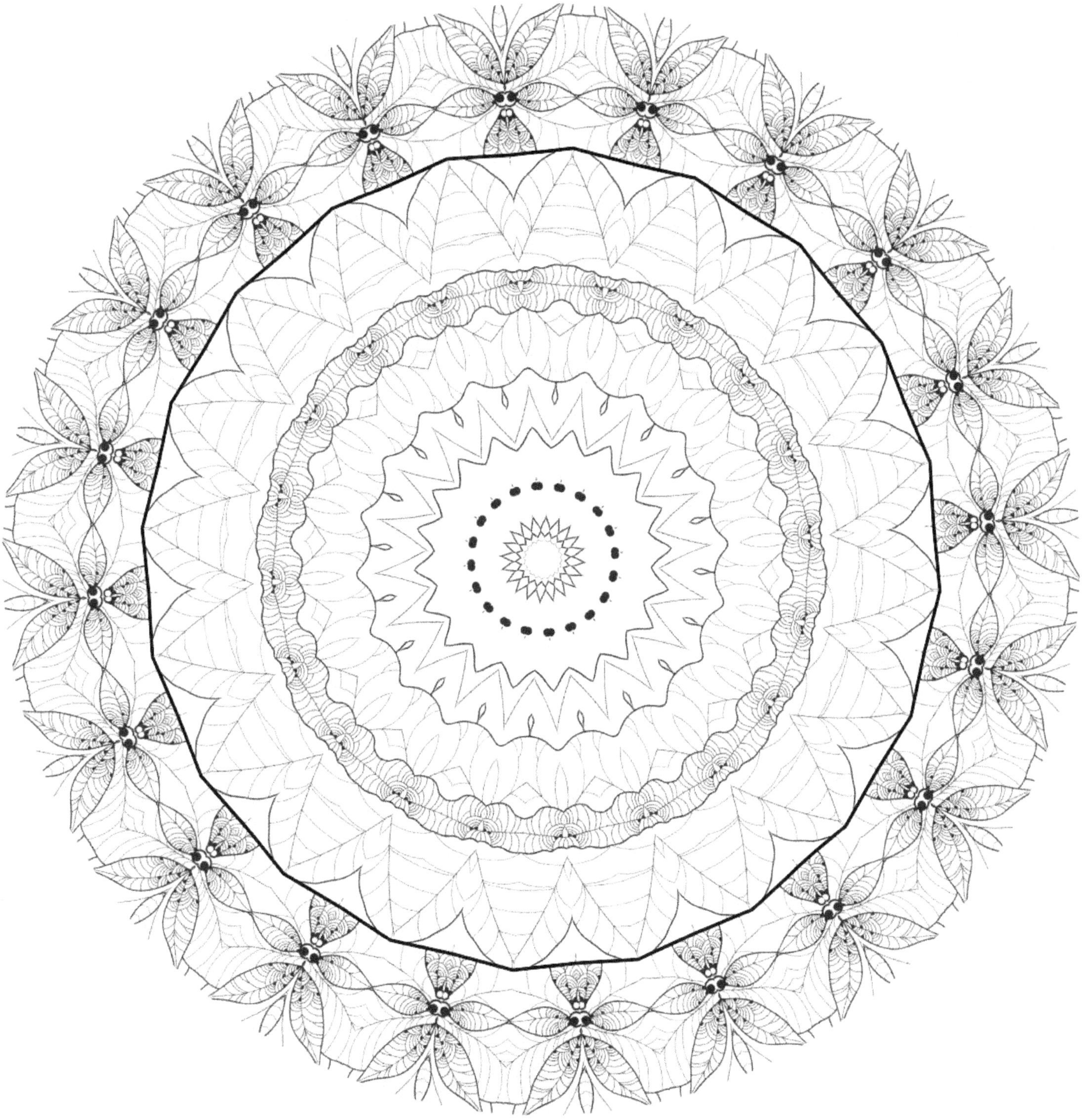

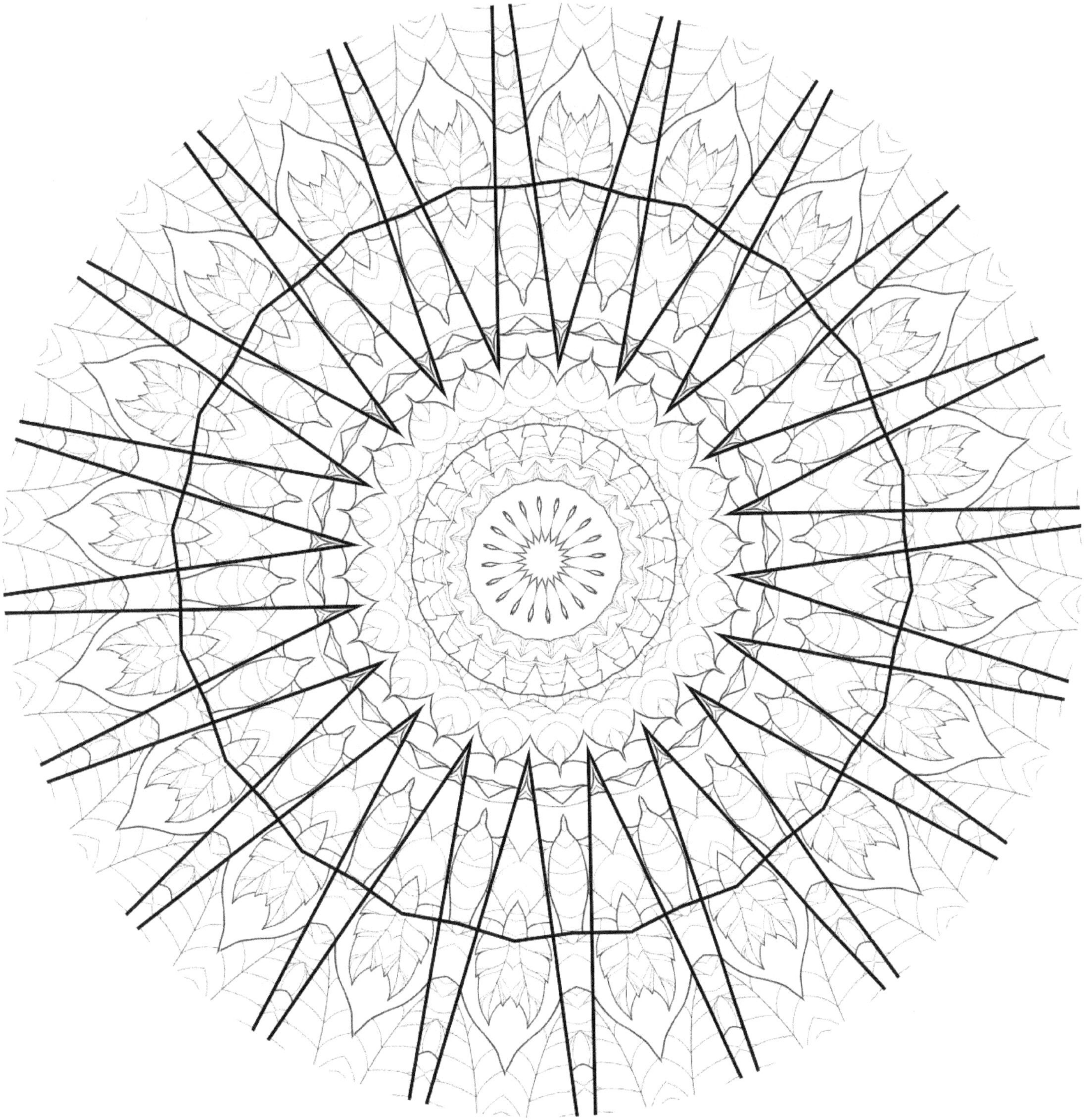

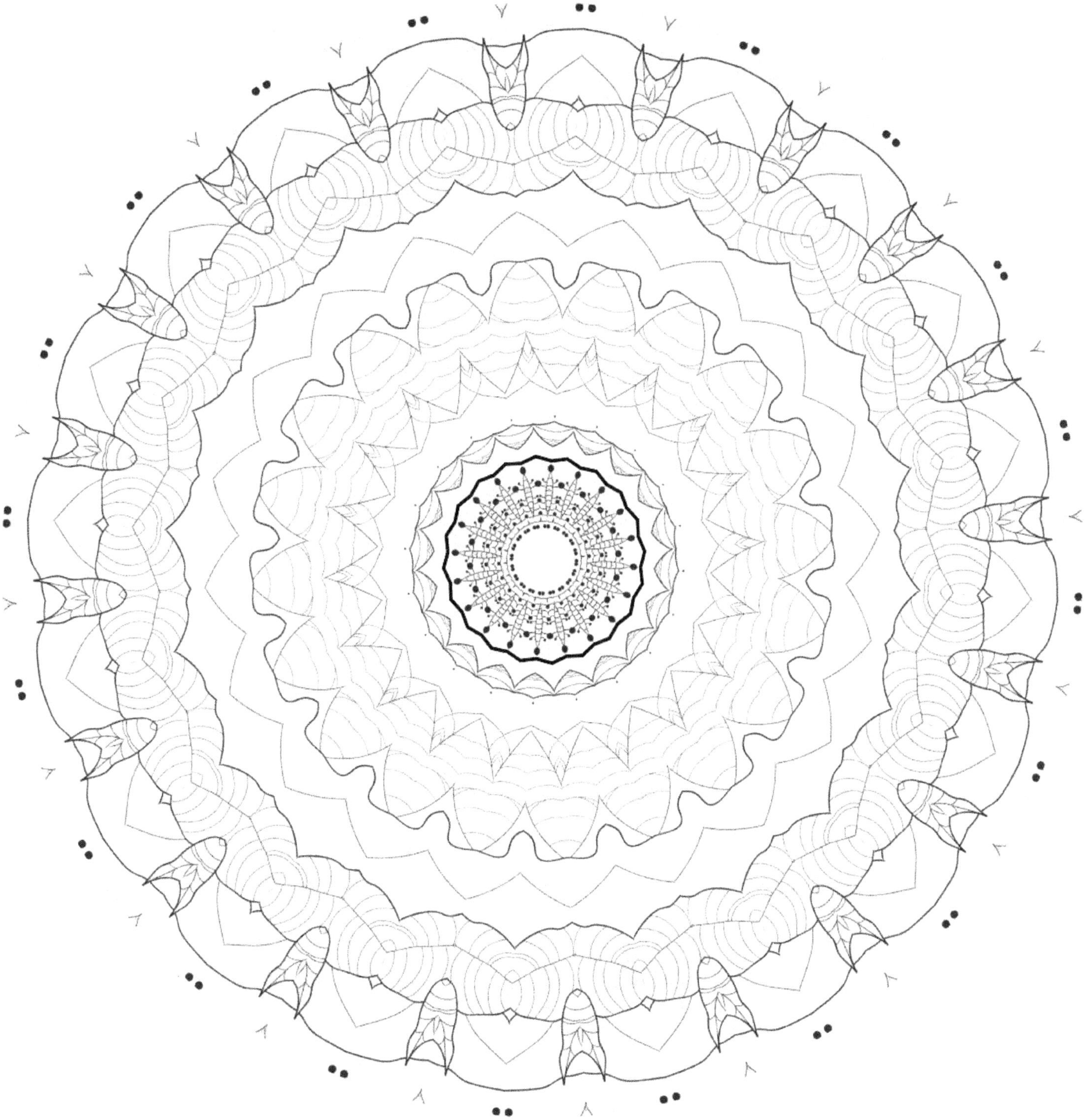

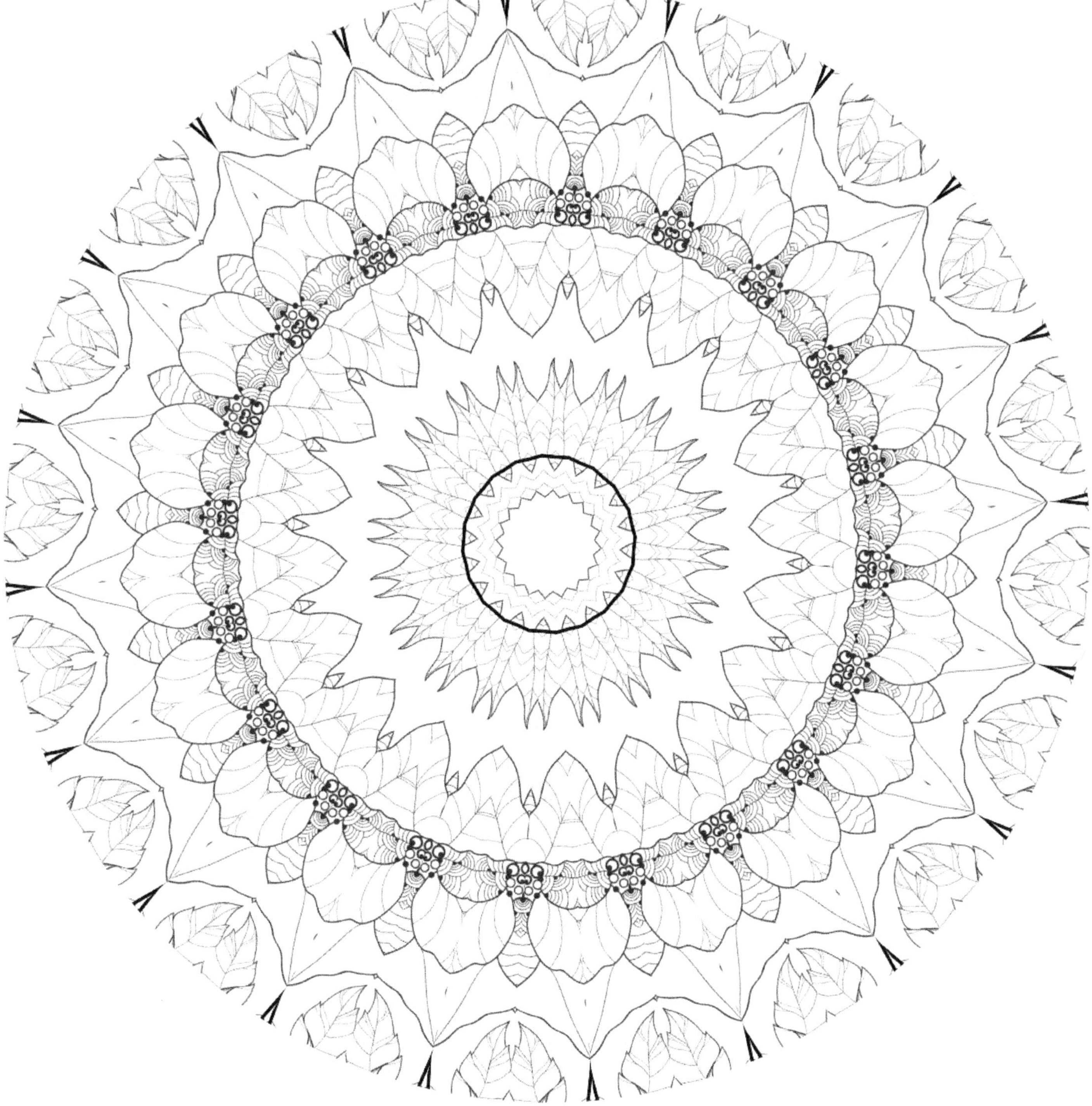

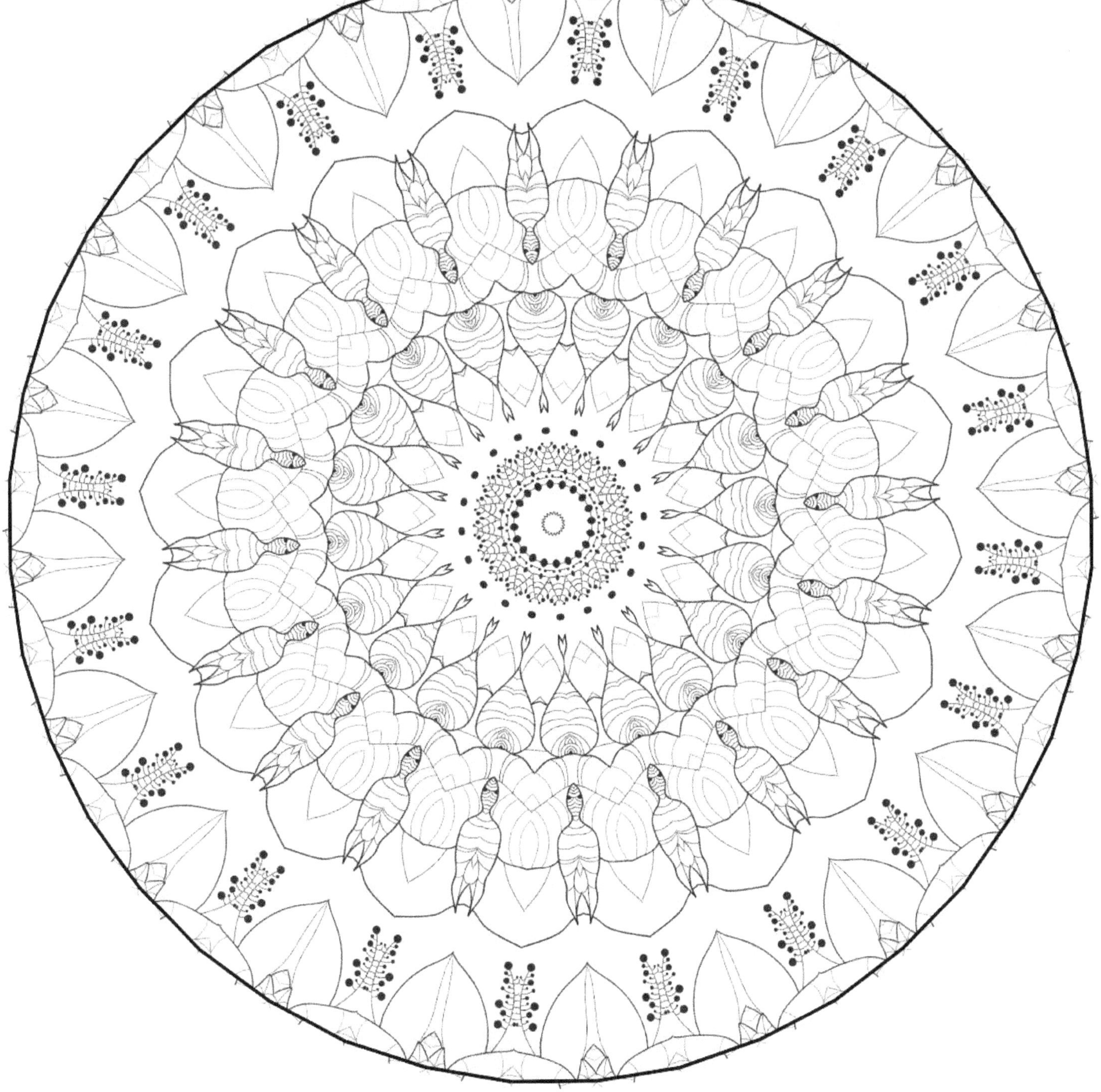

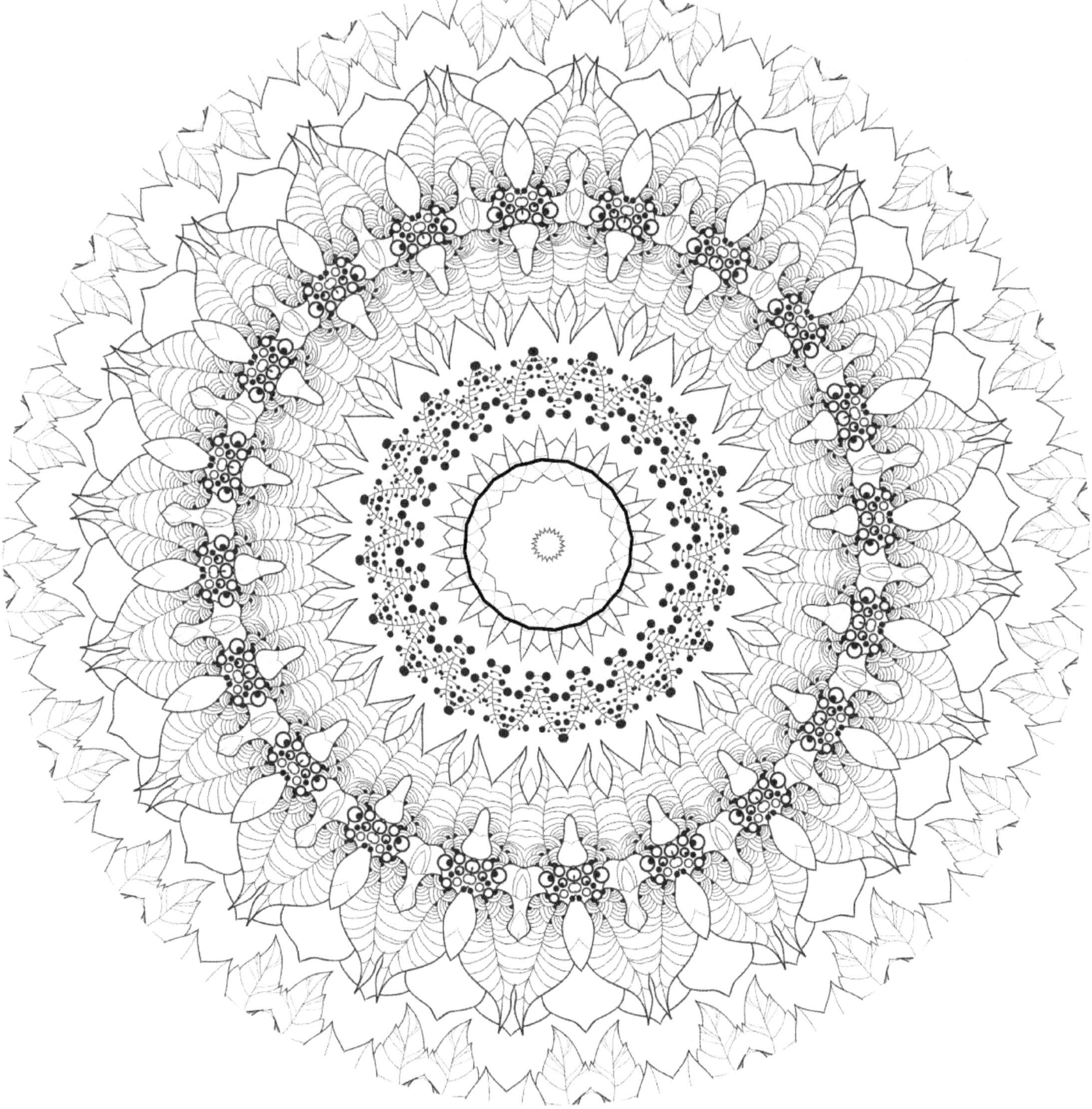

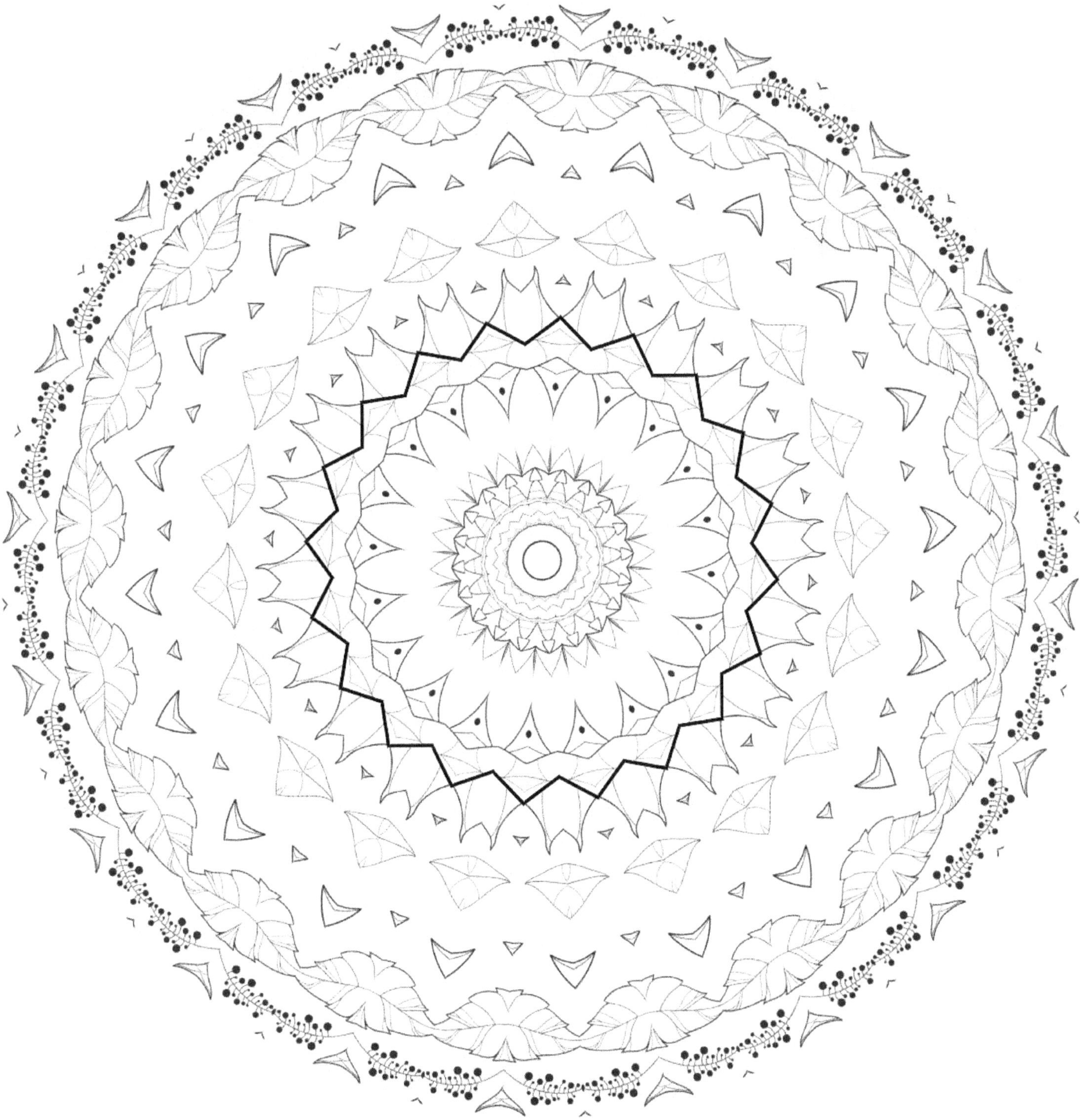

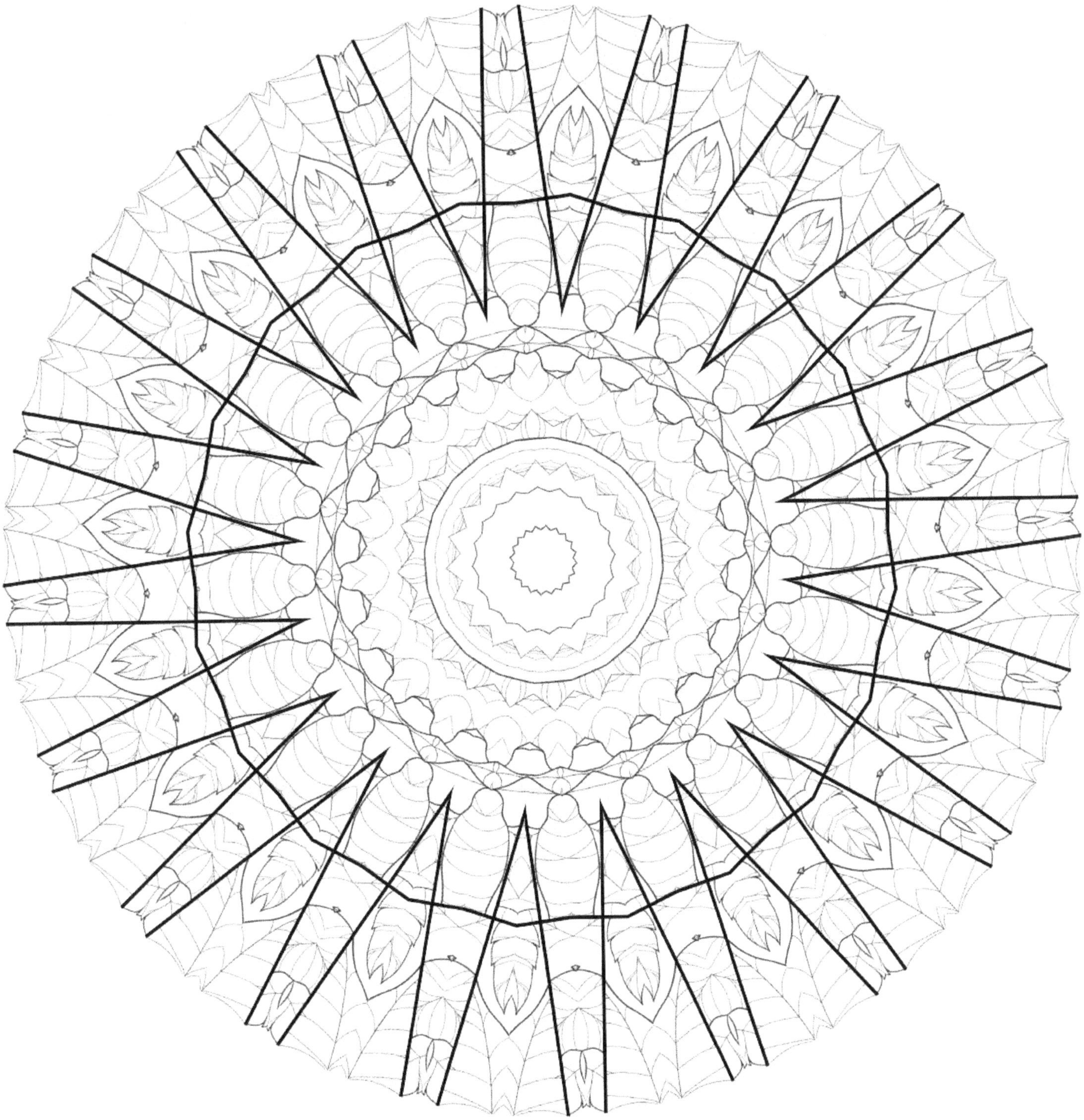

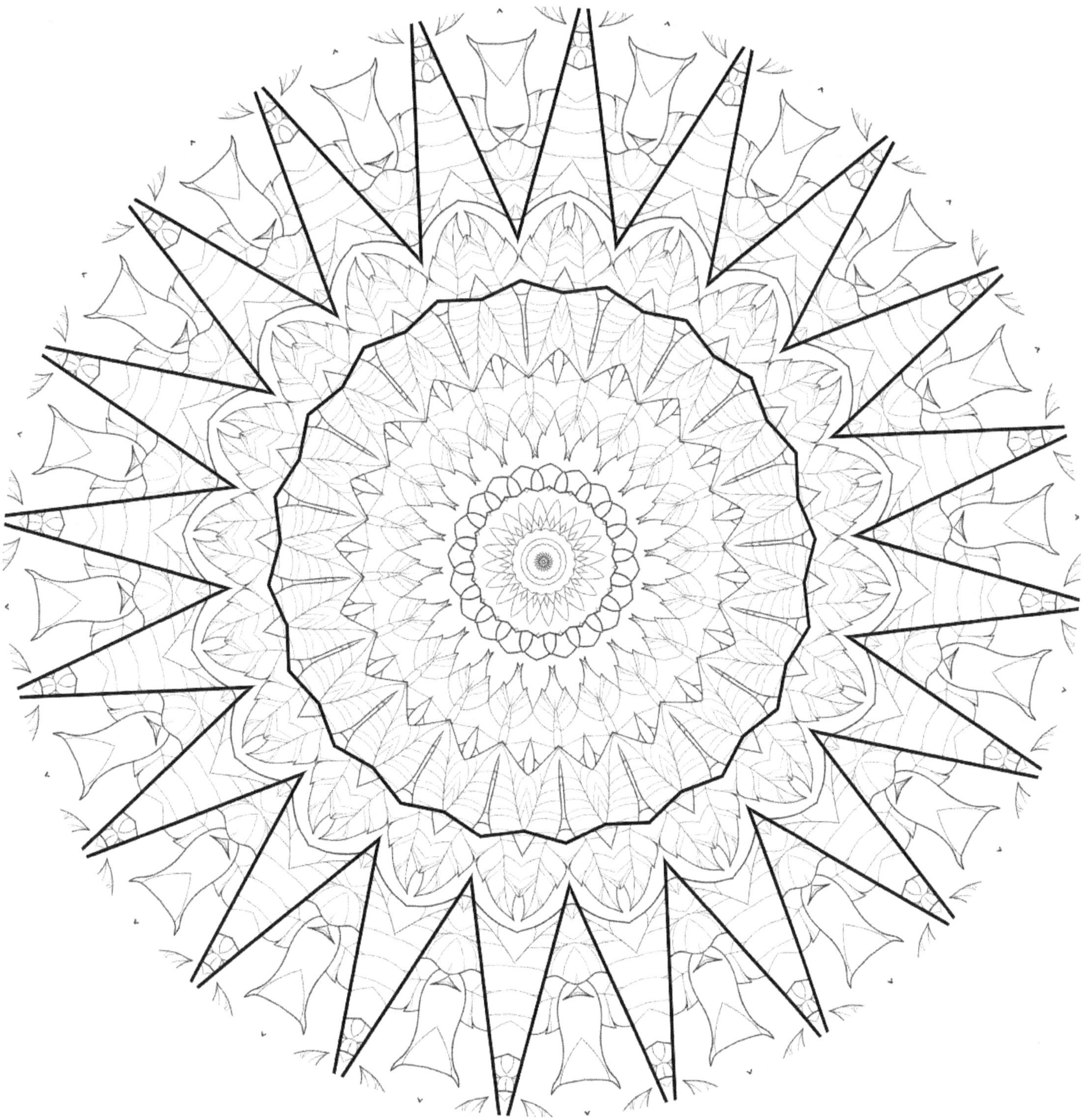

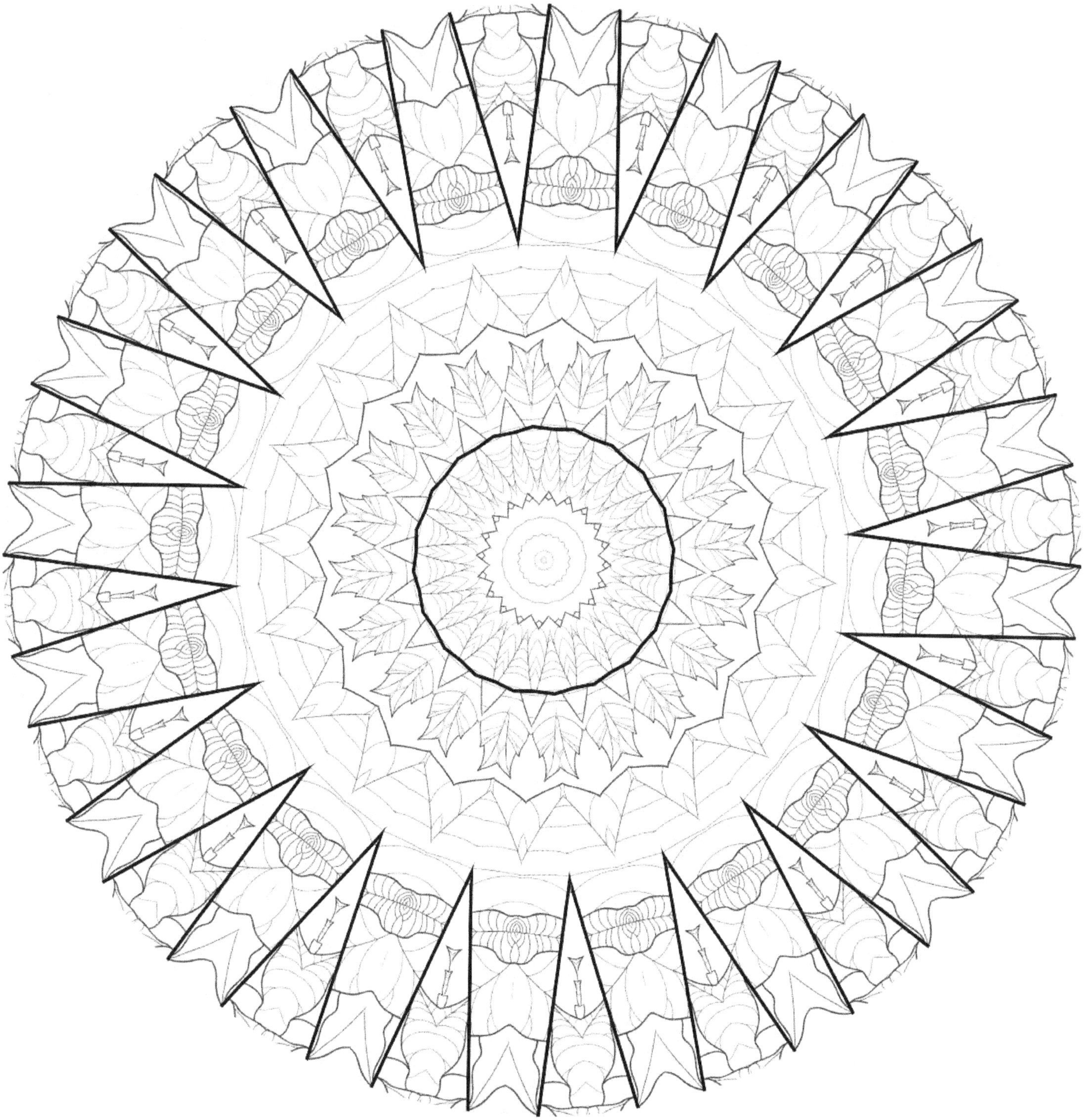

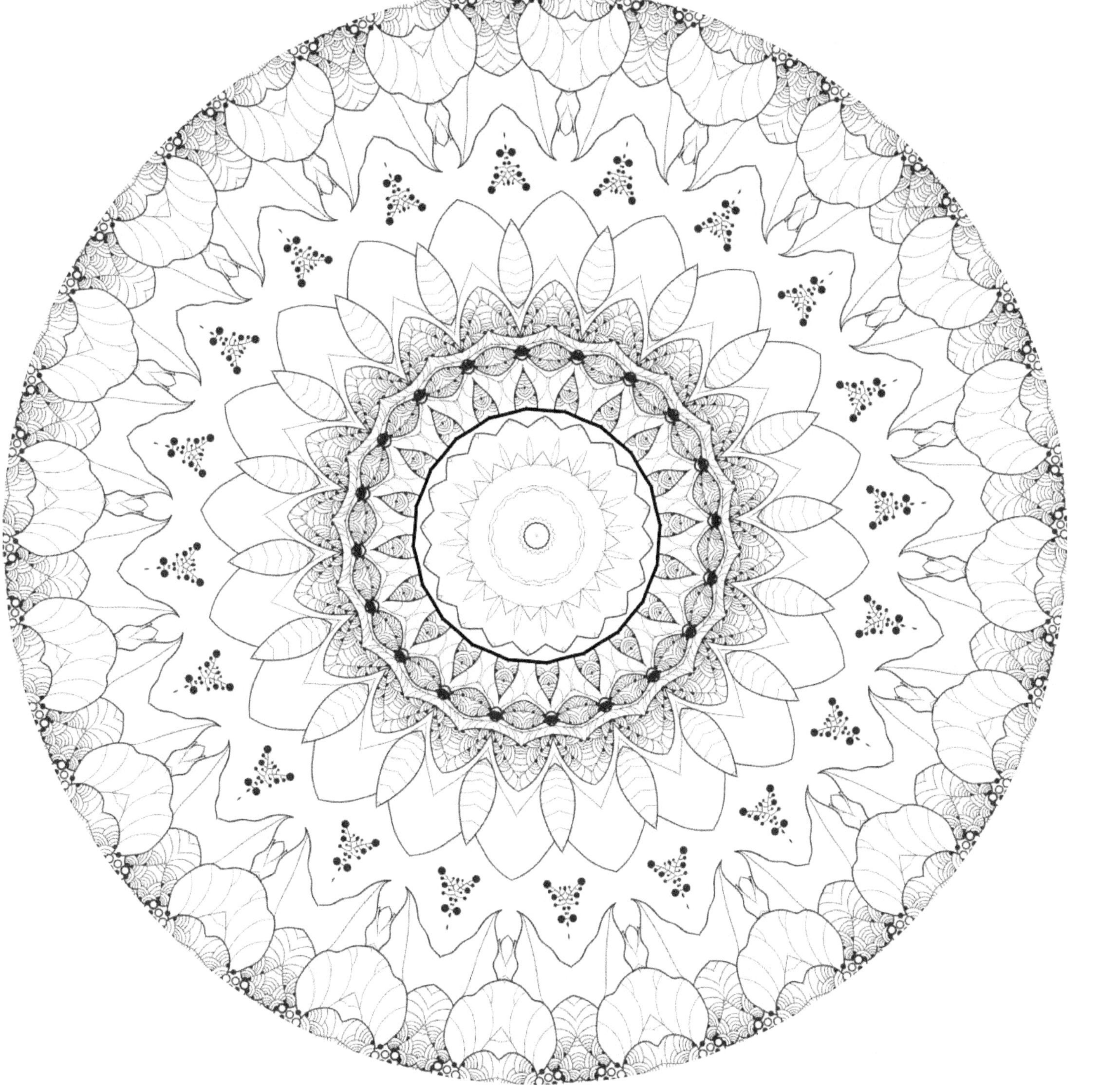

www.ingramcontent.com/pod-product-compliance
Lightning Source LLC
Chambersburg PA
CBHW081524220526
45467CB00010B/3039
* 9 7 9 8 6 9 1 7 4 3 6 8 9 *